"*Mother's Pearls* is an enlightenin
my own experiences and see Aha
new chapter brought to mind a si
upon, helping to remind me to tak
know an Aha moment at the time we're in it, but patience is the key until the true meaning is revealed."

—Lana Bertsch, President, Birchwood Productions Inc.

"With his insightful book Kevin Cottam presents 27 experiences that have the reader questioning her/his our life's journey, looking for the kernel of wisdom in each visitation. The cross-cultural sweep alone makes for an interesting read. Mother's Pearls is a treasure chest full of gems."

—J.Lafrentz, Engineer

"Each pearl shimmers with wisdom, creativity, and everyday practicality, while inviting me to recognize and maximize the pearls in my life."

—Pauline O'Reilly, Teacher

"The stories are so simple yet, they all have such powerful messages that really make you think about our conscious choices in every day life..."

—Ira Kita, Montessori Teacher

"To read a series of stories (the pearls), written from the heart, that shower you with truth and questions is but a unique and powerful experience. It is a guidebook and a support tool that can be picked up again and again, with some pearls read and re-read depending on your need or mood at that time. The Pearl's are an insight to life, being both biographically educational and some more formally educational. It is a gift that sits by my bed, alongside the Dalai Lama's Art of Happiness."

—Ailbhe Troubetzkoi, Communications Consultant

'We all have 'Aha' moments, times when the blur of our lives comes into clear focus, when the angles of the walls seem to bend, or the earth seems to shift under our feet with the new and powerful recognition of who we are and what our time on this planet is about.
In 'Mother's Pearl', the author has selected 27 of such moments that have altered the course of his life.
Moving, honest and from the heart, 'Mother's Pearls' is a true treasure – a beautiful necklace with its stones of wisdom, bright and timeless to treasure.'

—Vivienne Vermes, Author

'Marvellous Mey'

Aha

Mother's Pearls

You have graced our family with love, friendship, and full of smiles + light. We are forever grateful to have you in our lives. We only wish the best for you!

Kevin J Cottam

Love Kevin xxx 2013

CPMI
Creative Performance Mastery International Pte Ltd
Singapore, Singapore

Creative Performance Mastery International Pte Ltd.
Block 225
Lorong 8
Singapore, Singapore 310225

ISBN: 978-981-07-2242-5

Editor: Gordon Thomas • Designers: Julius Kiskis & Cory Wright
Proofreader: Bethanne Grabham • Cover photo: Bojan Tercon
www.kevincottam.com and www.ahamoments.us(blog)

Available from the National Library Board, Singapore Cataloguing-in-Publication Data

CREDITS
The author and publisher would like to thank the following for granting permission to use material in this book: SYDA Foundation for material featuring Swami Chidvilasananda.

Order this book or an ebook online at www.kevincottam.com or email info@kevincottam.com

Printed in Singapore, Singapore

20 19 18 17 16 15 14 13 12   2 3 4 5 6

Dedication

To my mother, Lily, for everything.

My dear friends Bojan and Robin, who believed in me throughout the challenges of writing this book.

My friend Nikos, who unfortunately didn't live long enough to write his own book.

My Guru, who has taught and assisted my awakening to *Aha* moments.

All my friends, family, and unknown people, who all live inside these stories and have created the space for awareness to happen.

"Be the change you want to see in the world."

Mahatma Gandhi

Contents

Acknowledgements

Thank you very much to the most generous and supportive Executive Producers who have assisted in making a personal dream, *Aha, Mother's Pearls* come to life.

Freedom Pearl
Robin and Bojan
Meg Mann and Mark Brown

Expansion Pearl
Randy Rae and Gary Lewis
Jay P. G. Wolfe
Jelle Boelen
Mirjam Pennings

Presence Pearl
Laura Alexandrou
Simone and Mark Alexander
Cristina Alvarez and Koen Suidgeest
Kathy Campbell
Carole, Marylou, and Seb
Anne H. Jensen Chatroux
Cathy Denny and David Anderson
Harm van der Endt
"Erika in Zurich"
Bruce Wallace Charles Grant
Ian, "a friend who believes in Kevin"
Sumaira Isaacs
David Kliman
Vincent Labeeuw
Janet Logan
Leslie Larch
Larry Peloso
Andrew A. W. Schuster and
Steven Tod Sparling
Judy Thomas
Martti Wichmann

Introduction

Live your pearls now, and use them to powerfully transform your life.

For a number of years, I lived in Europe and would routinely return to Canada each summer to visit my mother. Even at the advanced age of eighty-eight, she took great care to dress stylishly at all hours of the day, including breakfast. One hot summer morning, she appeared at the kitchen table wearing a double strand of pearls. My niece Launa exclaimed, "Oh Gran, you always look so good with your pearls!" We all smiled and laughed at this lovely moment, but for me it represented a profound realization. *Aha*, I thought, "'Mother's Pearls,' what a great name for my book."

That simple *Aha* moment triggered my desire to write this book. *Mother's Pearls* is a collection of twenty-seven short autobiographical chapters of *Aha* moments of realization. These moments in life often appear like a flash of light coming out of nowhere, from a voice or an image I may have seen, a sentence or phrase I may have heard, or voice deep from within. They can sometimes also appear completely contrary to what is happening at the time. They are a mystery really. Or are they? They may appear during a truly challenging and negative experience, which is just a face, or a "façade," if you like, as the beautiful pearl is sitting there behind the curtain waiting for us to discover it.

These moments are offered as gifts of messages, lessons, or knowledge. They are freely given to us and yet we often let them pass by, not acting upon them and letting them return into the ether. In *Mother's Pearls*, I invite you to discover your own pearls and what they mean and can do for you. It is here you can discover your truth, explore your journey, and fully celebrate your essence.

Through the art of storytelling, I have chosen to explore my *Aha* moments, my pearls. Storytelling is definitely not a new concept; it has existed since the beginning of time. As human beings, we discover our lives, our inner light, our worth, and more through the stories we hear and in turn relate to each other. All of this can lead to the development of our greatest human potential.

In telling my own stories, I have chosen pearls and oysters as metaphors for my journey. The pearls are the *Aha* moments of wisdom that have appeared to me throughout my life. The oysters are the locations where the pearls have occurred—they hold the pearls. I've had the rare opportunity and privilege to live in many different places and among numerous cultures, each of which has offered moments of revelation, learning, and inspiration—providing the pearls that, strung together, have so lovingly helped guide my way.

For me, discovering the bigger picture behind the story is what life is about. I hope you will also find the wisdom of each story by getting inside, behind, and on top of it. In turn, this new awareness will assist you to make more powerful decisions in your life. With these pearls, you will begin to see and experience how your life can transform with more self-confidence and self-worth.

Accepting and honouring my past, realizing what is present, and actively moving toward the future is a valuable truth. *Mother's Pearls* reflects some of the lessons on my journey that have led me to find the truth, my truth, and my reality. Through these pearls, I am now discovering how to perform more vibrantly and authentically from my heart. My hope is that, through this book, you can also find this awareness, comfort, and knowledge in your pearls.

Life today often feels comparable to a hurricane. When you are in the storm, it is extremely challenging to be objective. But if you simply stop for a minute, listen to the *Aha* moments, reflect on their teachings, and move toward the calm, interior eye of the storm (or simply step outside of it), you will begin to see the picture of your life in a much bigger way.

Take the time to really receive the *Aha* moments. Their gifts are there for you to move forward in your life with elegance and strength.

Imagine a closed tap. The water is being held back so tightly it cannot get through. Now when you open the tap, you allow the water to flow through. Allow yourself the fluidity and flexibility so you can loosen your grip on life a bit. Then, the messages or *Aha* moments will come, flowing through to you at the exact moment when you are ready to receive the pearls. Loosen up so you can hear, see, and feel the pearls that come with the *Aha* moments, which can appear at anytime in your life without any warnings at all. Be like a pirate and discover the treasure; but go farther to discover the treasure beneath the treasure.

As I have mentioned, my mother and her pearls gave me the title and metaphor for this book. Her love gave me the freedom to explore. My mother and my father gave me life, and I thank them for this. And now, I have also come to realize in a more profound way the meaning behind the saying, "We choose our parents and the life we come into." I am grateful and honoured to consider my own role in my creation.

I also want to thank all the people from around the world, from different cultural and professional backgrounds, who contributed to the creation of this book. They offered important perspectives and insights. Thanks specifically to Pauline O'Reilly, a fellow seeker in life, John LeFrenz, Jenny Tarrant, Kate, Lana, Sandy, Danny S., and Peter M. for providing valuable feedback.

Honour the Pearls that you are.
Honour the Oysters you have had.
Honour what you have created along the way.
Honour you and just be.
Be aware of that Aha moment as
You never know when it will appear.

Kevin J Cottam

Pearl • **Curiosity**

Oyster • **Melbourne, Australia**

*"Life
is without
meaning. You bring the
meaning to it. The meaning
of life is whatever you ascribe
it to be. Being alive is the
meaning."*

JOSEPH CAMPBELL

I recall, long ago, saying to myself:
I want to find my soul
My spirit.

When I was nineteen years old, I travelled to Australia, "Oz," to teach figure skating. Australia and figure skating may seem an unlikely match, and while it was not a great place for the sport, it was the beginning of a long journey called life. There, I experienced a "call to action," what American scholar Joseph Campbell would consider part of the mythical hero's journey. I didn't realize it at the time, but over the years I have come to know the importance of that moment.

For some time before that call, I had been itching to leave my home in Canada and travel. There was a discomfort, a restlessness inside me. A yearning voice kept gently speaking to me. I wanted to quit my training as a competitive skater to explore the world, as so many kids my age did. At that time, it was common to graduate from high school, grab a backpack, and take off. That was my call as well.

My journey began down under in Oz. It was the first time I had been so far away from my family and I only knew two Canadian skating coaches there. I experienced a roller coaster of emotions—I was happy at first with this new experience, but there were still lonely and disenchanted times.

In Oz, I found a place to stay in a charming rooming house by the sea on Ackland Street in St Kilda, a suburb of Melbourne. There were several nurses staying there from different parts of the world. One of them astutely felt it her duty to speak to me about culture shock, another taught me Buddhist ways and traditions, another about Christianity, and one even gave me cooking lessons. I was intrigued by the stories of these well-travelled women whose purpose in life was humanity with a capital "H."

I wondered if I would experience the stages of culture shock that they described. The first stage is when all is new and you love the place. The second stage is when a ferocious loneliness settles in and reality hits you to the very core with a voice inside saying, I miss home, family, friends, and familiarity. You begin to find fault in everything and everyone. It is a time to bolt. Then, during the third stage everything is beginning to be okay as your surroundings become more familiar. The final stage is when you become well adjusted and all is cool with the place and culture. This is when the staying power settles into the soul. Attaining this final stage takes a minimum of a year or even more, depending on your personality and support systems.

What were my support systems during these early stages? My father always said that if I got into trouble or felt lonely or lost I could always go to the church. My mother disagreed with this way of being because she felt that I should only rely on myself for support.

A short distance from the rooming house was a lovely Anglican church. I met the rector, Reverend Phil, who was a delight. I immediately took a liking to him and his family and they took me under their wings. He suggested I become confirmed in the Anglican Church. I had not been confirmed as a child, and through our discussions, I felt compelled to finish this part of my life's journey.

Reverend Phil guided me through my studies and soon I was confirmed and received my gift, a confirmation cross. I was very happy. Looking back on this experience, I sense now that this was the beginning of me being a born-again Christian. It seems unbelievable to me today, but at that time I was going through stage two of culture shock, so it was probably the best thing that could have happened. My mother had great concerns with me as I wrote home about God, Jesus, and the doctrine. My father, on the other hand, was supportive. They held two very different perspectives of the world.

One day, Reverend Phil suggested I get involved with a youth group. I did so and made some absolutely great friends and had a lot of fun participating with the singing groups, picnics, and spiritual sessions. It was a superb time that helped me through this very lonely stage of my life.

In the summer, I went with the church group to a camp in the Grampian Mountains in western Victoria for ten days. The Australian wilderness was magnificent. I felt like I was engaging directly with the land and the spirits.

At the camp, I met many new and cheery soulful people from all over the state of Victoria. The location was stunning, and I continued to learn about the countryside, the vegetation, nature, and the great outback. Our days were filled with hiking, playing games, swimming, singing, cooking, and lots of laughter. The evenings were spent in spiritual discussion. We even went on a three-day bush walk over the New Year's holiday. We dodged poisonous snakes, woke up to the yelling of the kookaburras, and saw a few kangaroos, all with the majestic eucalyptus trees towering over us.

Two nights before we were to leave the camp, I had heard from others that the last spiritual session would be the "big one." But no one would tell me what it would be about. My curiosity was piqued, what was the big secret?

The leader of our tent took us in his VW bus and drove into the pitch-black and starry night. There must have been about six to eight of us crowded into the van. He began with the talk. It was about sex. Yes, sex, and how incorrect and sinful it was before marriage. Casual sex was just not right, even with your loved one. He also spoke about the correctness of heterosexuality and the opposition to homosexuality. I recall being taken aback at the forcefulness of this discussion. It just seemed so contrary to all other teachings on kindness, giving from the heart, and seeing all as a reflection of oneself.

I remember he began the talk by asking us about our thoughts on premarital sex and if we had made love already. A couple were too shy to say anything and I sensed they had already had premarital sex, but denied it. Others had not had sexual intercourse and said so. When it came to me, I just told the truth.

Yes, I said, I had made love to a couple of women and thought there was nothing wrong with it. I felt it to be a natural extension of our nature, our being, and our evolution. Being married was not a licence for me to then partake of the fruit that life was already presenting to me. I felt when I had made love it was coming from my heart and not from my lustful desires of a youthful teenager.

Well, apparently I was wrong in their eyes and I could feel the tension change from everyone in the van. I could sense the heat rising. It was ready to take off. I felt at the time I was made to feel like a true sinner.

I was appalled at what I instantly perceived as hypocrisy. I was doing no harm to anyone, I was telling the truth, I was honest, and that, obviously, was just as punishable. I was told there was scripture that identified my actions as sinful and improper. I remember my stubbornness, but I eventually succumbed to their suggestions and said I would consider the scripture, even though I was doubtful I would change my ways.

It was strange how I felt about their reaction. I suddenly felt something just didn't fit inside of my being. I felt isolated and alone for the rest of the trip. I felt a little like I had reverted back into stage two of culture shock. I was in a state of confusion, unhappiness, and, yet again, loneliness.

The next day, I was sitting on the lakeside beach and my leader came to me with scripture to show me where it spoke about acts of the flesh and marriage. I realized he was trying to convince me that my beliefs, which I sensed from my heart, were wrong, fundamentally wrong, although I was not judging him or the others for their beliefs.

Something triggered inside of me. It was not just this discussion, but

I realized that there seemed to be so much doctrine that just didn't make sense for me. Perhaps I was beginning to see a bigger picture of the world. Was I getting an actual taste of what growing up and culture shock were truly about? I then felt as if I had gone into a time warp; everything went into slow motion. I looked around and saw such wonderful people and I was curious about what were they were really thinking. Were they really honest with their beliefs, values, and actions? And, in fact, was I?

I sensed I needed to follow all of them or none of them. I sensed a deeper calling that said this has been wonderful experience, but now I need to discover on my own. This was the kick-start of something greater. It was my "call to action." I wanted to know the diverse possibilities of life. I wanted to really learn and discover how the lives of other people ticked in the world.

The time in the Grampians was still fruitful for me. My bush walk through valleys and up the mountains also gave me time to ponder and expand my ideas. I reflected that the loneliness of stage-two culture shock is actually the valley of learning. We need to rest and savour this valley of learning, and use this opportunity to be curious. From there, we can emerge as stronger people who are able to proceed back up the mountain, to stages three and four.

After all these years, I see that this period in my life in Oz was more than just culture shock of moving to a place, but a shock to my inner journey as well. Those nurses were catalysts to change that I would not be aware of for many years to come. These situations redirected my conceptualization of the world and people. It was a tremendous learning experience. My father and mother were both correct in their advice to me during this time in Australia; they simply held different points of view. I am thankful for this experience that taught me about the bigger picture of culture shock and where it was leading me. It shocked me into full action.

I never made it to stage four in Oz. Unfortunately, my experience down under ended a year before its time when my father suddenly died of a heart attack. When it happened, my mother said, "Don't come home yet, but continue to travel and experience life for a little longer." I did just that. This was the beginning of another part of my journey. In fact, in the traditional sense of the hero's journey, this was also part of my call to action, and the rest that followed has all been learning.

This is when growth began.
This is when the seeds began to open.
This is when the river really began to flow.
This is where choice comes in.
Get curious.

After saying my thanks and good-byes to my friends and Christian brothers and sisters in Oz, I heard this voice inside saying,

'I want to find my soul',
My true soul,
My spirit.
That is my quest in life.
The mountain is high,
The valley is low,
Shaped to support you
Like a cradle.
Learning takes place there.

Take a step, two steps, three
Out of the valley
And gleefully rise
Up the mountain with
Power, strength
And a chest full of Air
That sends you into flight.
Your call to action has been heard and
Accepted with fullness of the heart.
'I want to find my soul',
My true soul,
My spirit.

DISCOVERY

When was your "call to action"? ~ Are you curious about life? ~ How important is it for you to be curious in life? ~ What would this curiosity do or give to you? ~ Take a moment to contemplate your curiosities in your life and how you manifest this in your daily activities. Maybe it is time to shock yourself with your wisdom and take action on this shimmering pearl.

Pearl • **Fear**

Oyster • **Westkerke, Belgium**

*"If you
want to make
peace with your enemy,
you have to work with your
enemy. Then he becomes your
partner."*

NELSON MANDELA

A*ha* moments can appear at the least expected times or periods in our lives, in the oddest places, and in some of the most bizarre situations. They are exciting moments, yet they can be simultaneously disorienting and confusing. Being receptive to the *Aha* moment—whenever and however it arrives—is very rewarding and can be a transformative experience.

One late summer day, I was peacefully walking along the beach in northern Belgium with some friends when suddenly the thought "what is fear?" popped into my head. To this day, I have no idea what prompted this question in my mind. It was very odd, as I was not in a dangerous or uncomfortable situation at all, but rather the opposite, I was in a blissful state. But there it was, sitting in my conscious mind, begging to be seen and heard. In fact, it was as if I was watching fear, not from an emotional or intellectual state, but rather from a distance; it appeared as an entity, a concept, or maybe even a personality.

We all have experienced fear in many ways. Fear can be our greatest paralyzer if we allow it to be. It dresses up in different clothes and wears different masks, but behind all that camouflage, it is the face of fear, the potential of fear, that holds us back. It can send us into downward spirals, smacking us around emotionally, mentally, physically, and spiritually. It can also hold us back from living our dreams and performing at our highest potential.

We can, however, respond to those negative forces constructively and with courage. On that day at the beach, I was confronted with a different image of fear, it had a gentle and kind face that led and encouraged me to come closer.

I continued walking in silence along the beach with my friends as the waves of the North Sea gently washed against the long sandy shore. Children and their parents were flying kites of many shapes and colours; people frolicked in the water and built sand castles. Sailboats gracefully caught the wind and moved across the English Channel. Happiness, joy, and freedom permeated the atmosphere.

Surrounded by beauty, my blissful state was being interrupted by the image of fear in my mind. I was confused. Why was this notion of fear choosing to visit my thoughts on such a deep spiritual and intellectual level? What was happening? I decided to explore my curiosity.

I sat down quietly with my friends and gazed at the North Sea. In my mind, an open doorway appeared before me. On the other side of it, fear was sweetly smiling and beckoning me forward. It did not have a horrific appearance or sensibility, but rather embodied a sense of expansion and learning. In my mind, I then looked behind me and saw another form of fear. It was the kind that holds you back, stops you in your tracks, and limits you and keeps you in a comfort zone that ultimately leads to those downward spirals.

In front of me, on the other side of the doorway, fear held out its hand and said, "Come with me and use me to expand, learn, grow, transform: let me be your potential." Yet behind me, I could hear the other, menacing face of fear trying to taunt me, saying, "You can't do that. Now I've got ya, you fool, just the way I want ya, you're mine now." But this face of fear behind me was unsuccessful in its attempts to scare me; in fact, it wasn't scary at all.

To my surprise, this apparition also gave me a sense of happiness. This time, an image of fear was presented to me unadorned with negativities. I felt joy. I felt smiles come over me. Most importantly, I felt a lightness, a weightlessness within in my body. I was seeing fear in a new way, with a new face and with new colour and new texture. The new face of fear was pure light, not dark. It was positive, not negative. The fear I saw before me was compassionate and from the heart, filled with new possibility, new hope.

As I sat on the bench, taking in this new concept fear, I thought I would see if I could put it into action. The first thing that came to mind was the writer's block that had plagued me for some time.

Several months before, I had eagerly begun writing this book after many years of thinking about it. I was moving along with great intent and even asked people to hold me to task on writing each chapter. But after about two months of writing, I abruptly stopped. I became afraid. I started to make excuses. I put everything else in my way of completing it and just froze.

As I contemplated the apparition of the open doorway and the image of light versus dark, I realized the dark side of fear that was standing behind me was stopping me from writing. I couldn't get myself past it to continue to write. It looked so evil and unwelcoming. It would hurl nasty names and comments at me like, "You failure, you can't write, why would anyone read this?" Every time I tried to dodge it or push it out of the way, the scary fear seemed to outwit me. I was literally trapped in a cage of fear.

What would happen if I viewed fear as permeated with light as it stood before me at the door? Would I start writing again? An inner voice said, "You have nothing to fear but fear itself. With which face of fear do you want to complete your book?" The inner voice was actually inviting me to test myself to live my wants, desires, and dreams. It appeared to be egging me on and playing games with me.

Writing this book was not a life and death choice, even though fear may have made me believe so. This time something was different. Fear seemed to become a friend, not a foe. *Aha*!

That day on the beach, with the good face of fear holding my hand as a lover would, I decided that it was time to walk into the light, take my pen, and write again. I suddenly realized that procrastination was not serving my dreams.

When I returned home, I reflected on my experience of fear and my commitment to continue my writing. I saw more clearly the implications of not writing and postponing my work.

I walked into the light fear with passion and commitment. I thanked the dark fear for the lessons it had shown me. I completed the first draft of my book three weeks later, without looking back.

We all have stories of fear. We all have relationships that have been affected by fear. Do you allow your life to be run on fear and limit you, or do you want to live a life filled with possibilities?

You never know when an *Aha* moment will strike. So be alert, and if you miss it, don't fret; it will most likely try to get your attention again at different times and places. You will eventually hear its voice and listen.

Embrace your fears and turn them into action and light. We all can develop a new relationship with fear—a much healthier and energetic one!

DISCOVERY

What do you do when you are trapped in a cage of fear? ~ Take some time to reflect on how you deal with fear and what it does to your life, your potential, your performance, and notice how others see you react to your fear. Give fear some space and really look at it as a friend and see how it can assist you in your growth, actions, and solutions. How can fear serve your life?

3RD PEARL

Pearl • **Expectations**

Oyster • **Toronto, Canada**

*"When
one door closes
another opens. But we
often look so long and so
regretfully upon the closed door
that we fail to see the one that
has opened for us."*

ALEXANDER GRAHAM BELL

Some years ago, I was sitting on a psychiatrist's couch in Toronto, spilling my guts over a rather traumatic event that I couldn't seem to sort out. For most of the session, the psychiatrist listened and didn't say a word. Suddenly, a profound statement came from her mouth: "What did you expect?"

I was dumbfounded, taken aback, speechless. I thought, *Aha*, what did I expect? Good point. I had spent many hours getting to this little piece of wisdom with her. It signified a turning point and an ultimate resolve that brought my time in therapy to a close.

Expectations plague most of us many times each day. I once read an article entitled "The Tyranny of Expectations" that describes this pearl beautifully. It discusses the difference between expectations, which are based in the future, as opposed to possibilities, which are based in the present. The former often leads to unhappiness and a weaker state of being, while the latter often leads to happiness, strength, and power.

I include "expectation" as a pearl, but not as an attribute for us to aspire to attain, but rather as a positive tool for what it can teach us.

This is why I was sitting on the psychiatrist's couch. I was once the choreographer for a world figure skating champion. I was away in Australia on holiday while he defended his Canadian championship title, which would qualify him to compete for the next world championships. He won the Canadian title, but barely, due to his lackluster performance.

What had happened? The year after he had won his first world championship, celebrity status kicked in. Rightfully so, he wanted to take advantage of most invitations that came his way. However, he lost focus of training and the new competitive season. So one may say, "What did he expect when he didn't train that hard or efficiently?"

When I returned to Canada to work with him prior to the upcoming world championships, I found an uncertain, frightened, and demoralized skater. I had never ever seen him like this. He was always positive, uplifting, and full of life. Seeing his new condition, spectators, skaters, and officials repeatedly questioned what I was going to do with him. I replied, "It is only my role to choreograph and train his programs, nothing else. The rest is for his coach to deal with."

The first day we worked on the ice, I saw that he was unable to land many of his jumps or get through his programs with any display of finesse or stamina. It was a sad sight. I was between a rock and a hard place. I couldn't work on choreography because all the choreography in the world was not going to help him if he couldn't land his jumps and other technical elements. I sensed many eyes were focused on me to help this guy out of his predicament, as it didn't appear his coach was doing much to change the situation. The skater wanted to improve—it was in his eyes, in his heart. He was like a little frightened puppy that couldn't seem to find his way home.

Later in the day, I went to talk to him about setting up our next lesson. In desperation, he said, "I can't do this. I don't know how. I won't win. I have never been like this and don't know what to do." Tears came to his eyes. Suddenly, his coach came rushing off the ice and said in a rather brisk tone, "This looks like a conversation I should be involved in." I said we were just talking about lesson plans, but the coach seemed displeased with what he had witnessed.

That night, I had dinner with an Australian coach who was visiting. We talked about this situation. I explained that it wasn't my role to council the skater through his predicament, but she repeatedly insisted that it was my duty, regardless.

The next day, I got up and got out of my ego's way and surrendered to the task at hand. My mantra was my duty to him, no matter what the outcome would be. So I met him in the morning and said, "Here's the plan. You may hate me by the end of the week and yell obscenities to me, but I am going to train you, and train you hard. I am going to skate after you and talk to you encouragingly while you go through your programs until you get it right." He agreed to the plan.

We dug in hard together and trained when his coach was not around. In six days he made enormous strides. He was back on track and mentally strong. He was landing his jumps and technically on target.Smiles reappeared on his face. A new energy and confidence filled his body. His heart was open again with possibilities. When I left to return to Toronto, he said, "I know I can do it now."

Expectations were high for this talented skater. It was kind of like betting on a racehorse. In retrospect, what we did during that week was focus on the possibilities, not the expectations, so that he could regain his confidence, power, and strength. This was important so that he could move toward a goal with a renewed determination.

A few weeks later, he won the world championship. It was a glowing performance. Considering where he was just a few weeks prior, he outperformed himself, amazed others with his comeback, and consequently learned a valuable lesson.

I subsequently had a meeting with his coach to discuss plans for the next season. The coach harshly told me that he no longer wanted to work with me. Stunned, my heart fell to the ground and my ego came racing back with a burning sense of anger.

I was embarrassed. I took it personally and couldn't believe his lack of gratitude. I walked away shaken and lost, not knowing what to say.

This was the turning point that ultimately sent me to the psychiatrist. I just couldn't cope with this bruise to my ego. I had to work this out, and after much work and many hours of therapy, the *Aha* moment appeared, "What did I expect?" An extremely good question!

It has taken many more years, but I now look back at this situation and realize what an important discovery it presented me. From the time we wake up in the morning till we go to bed at night, we are creating expectations, some small, some very large. Expectations are linked to an outcome and our deeply set values. What come with expectations are rigid and locked ideas, images, and feelings that you think you must live up to.

We are so wonderfully creative. We envision our desires, but then they sometimes get put away on the back burner, in the unconscious. Some expectations may happen exactly as we wish, but how many don't? Most are not at all like what we had originally pictured or shaped inside of our heads. How does this make us feel in our mind, body, and soul?

Most of us are rarely happy with the outcomes of our expectations. The locked images we create stay the same, but in the process of realizing them, many other experiences and situations will reshape and create new possibilities for the final outcome of our expectations. However, our unconscious mind has a challenging time to shift the original images. Hence, this rigid lock does not take the opportunity to shift and allow the flow of change and new possibilities, even if they are in a more positive or advantageous direction.

Here is where being flexible and allowing possibilities enters the scene. Along the way toward the expectation, give yourself permission to live in the present with the possibilities, which can make the outcome grow, flourish, and sprout into something better.

I am not saying don't have expectations in life or business, but what I am suggesting is to be less rigid in our idea of the outcome. This inflexibility often occurs because, unconsciously, certain values may be at play and we get stuck in the original image that doesn't fit with the final outcome. See the many wonderful aspects that surround achieving that outcome, as that is where the wisdom is. The wisdom is not in the outcome, but the journey toward it.

In my situation, I had expected something negative to happen because I stepped over what were my perceived duties. However, I did not see any changes coming forth from the current situation at the time, and took a bold risk and heartfully chose my duty to help my skater. This led to the possibilities for the skater to experience a shift in his outcomes. And, it allowed me to be in the present, rather than focusing rigidly on the outcome.

So when the psychiatrist asked, "What did you expect?" She was speaking about the behaviour of the coach in this situation. What made me think the result would be any different than those of my previous experiences with him? I had hoped and even created the possibility in the back of my mind that the coach would rise above his ego and recognize the value I was creating for his skater. The problem was I was creating this expectation without the coach being part of it. I could not expect anything else, as the coach was simply responding as he normally would.

The opportunity to learn from this situation has been rich. The biggest lesson I learned is that if we must set expectations, allow them to be soft, flexible, and fluid. Let them be enhanced by possibilities, which will make them more wonderful. Allow your values to be free and not so rigid, but still live by them authentically. You never know what will be the real image of the outcome because so many different processes along the way must come together to make it happen.

Ultimately, that skater and I worked together again, but this time with different intentions, objectives, and outcomes. It was a gratifying and happy ending, one that was completely unexpected!

DISCOVERY

Do you have expectations? ~ Reflect on a time when you reached an outcome and it was not exactly as you wanted or expected it to be. What happened along the way that didn't allow your expectation to be exactly as you envisioned? ~ What would happen if you would loosen your hold on the original image and allow for learning and possibilities along the way to make the experience richer? ~ Give yourself a chance to experience the unexpected.

4TH PEARL

Pearl • **Breathe**

Oyster • **Toronto, Canada**

"When
the breath
wanders the mind also
is unsteady. But when the
breath is calmed the mind
too will be still, and the yogi
achieves long life. Therefore,
one should learn to control the
breath."

SVATMARAMA, HATHA YOGA PRADIPIKA

One muggy summer evening, I was sitting at the dining room table having dinner with my partner. At one point she said to me, "Every time you see Ming Tu, you come home different. Why is this?" Her voice didn't reveal delight, but rather some bitterness and edge. I didn't understand her question. I said, "Different? How so?" She replied, "I don't know. You are just different and I don't like it very much. It makes me uneasy because you seem so distant." I could sense her "dis-ease" with this situation and I became stressed over this conversation.

I couldn't put my finger on it at that time, but I have come to realize it was my breathing; there was definitely a major shift in my breathing pattern after my visits with Ming Tu. It had dropped deeper into my body and became slower, calmer, more open and much richer.

I began to think about what this difference could mean. I began thinking about how I was before, during and after meeting with my friend. A devout Buddhist, Ming Tu had an immense presence for a small man. I sensed a deep change within whenever we spent time together.

Ming Tu was an opera stage manager by profession and monk-like in appearance. When I first met him, I sensed something very different about him and I became curious. We struck up a friendship immediately.

One day I had tea with him at his house. His home had the most wonderful air of serenity, love, and gentleness. The colours of the home were soft and it embodied a sense of feng shui. He had a serene, beautiful little Zen garden with a fountain of running water, and a lovely Buddha with old incense sticks and some greenery and small stones surrounding it. This garden was one of the places he meditated and there was truly something different about the energy in this space and indeed throughout the entire house.

His home held a sense of being that I had not experienced since visiting Thailand many years before. The balance and centeredness of the space was present and touching me at a deeper level than I realized.

When Ming Tu spoke, he was humourous, vivacious, and stimulating in a very grounded way. Whenever he was busy on stage, he did it with a flow, happiness, and grace. It seemed that nothing threw him off and his energy transcended the space around him.

I became more restful in his presence, calmer, more center, and very peaceful. I felt a wonderful light breath of energy flowing through my body. I remembered what bliss this was, but I was also wrapped up in my thoughts to truly grasp what was happening.

During this period of my life, I had begun to tentatively explore yoga, spirituality, and other practices. What I experienced through my visits with Ming Tu was something that I wanted for myself, but I didn't know how to get it. I have come to realize that even though I sensed this blissful state, I was definitely not yet ready for such deep spiritual work.

The centering that I sensed inside was definitely apparent to my partner. She sensed a shift in me, and although it was positive, the change made her somewhat frightened and insecure.

Over time, I came to learn that breathing is in itself a centering technique. It is a life practice which can assist us to move through stressful situations and give us more mind control over who we are and what we want to be. It can also give us more focus and take us deeper to the truth within us. It is a journey to the heart. It is a necessity if you want to lead a purposeful, engaged life. And, although it is the most essential aspect of life, breathing is often misunderstood.

Breathing leads to presence. Honouring the breath of life is what inspires us. We inspire the breath of life. The inspiration leads to a center nature, if we so wish to focus on this result. Have you ever focused on your breathing? When tuned into it, you begin to find the depth of your being. Breathe deep into your belly.

As human beings, we all consciously, or perhaps unconsciously, search for this zone that creates a calm and happy nature. Centering assists us to make this leap of faith. Before we can do anything in life, it is helpful to be center as we become clearer in our mental, emotional, physical, and spiritual intelligence. We gain clarity in a warm and meaningful way.

Eventually, Ming Tu left Toronto and I never saw him again. Prior to his departure, I asked him to leave his address and contact details. He said something like, "If we are to come together again, that is our destiny. If not, our encounter has been a great lesson in life." This was not the answer I wanted, but it was what I had to live with. I was left with a deep sense of sadness.

I now realize after all these years that Ming Tu taught me a profound lesson. In retrospect, he was teaching me to be center in the present moment, to breathe with awareness, and allow grace to fill my heart. At that time, I chose not to follow his wisdom. It was only years later when I realized what he had taught me that the divine appeared loud and clear. Eureka, *Aha*, I awoke out of ignorance, and now know the reason he came into my life.

Aha moments are magical because although they are often immediately startling, their meanings sometimes take a long time to become clear. Be patient, remain alert, and breathe gently.

My dinner may have not gone well that evening with my partner, but now I can say thank you, Ming Tu. You led me to the realization of this magnificent pearl, Breathe.

DISCOVERY

Have you ever consciously focused on your breathing? ~ As you sit at your desk or in front of the TV, as you move around or stand still, and as you get into conversations that are stressful or harmonic, how is your breathing different? ~ Explore the possibilities of becoming more aware of your breathing patterns and ways to breathe more deeply, taking full inhales and exhales. Sense how it can change your state of being and performance in life. Focus on your breathing.

Pearl • **Gratitude**

Oyster • **Kanyakumari, India**

"To
educate yourself
for the feeling of gratitude
means to take nothing for
granted, but to always seek out
and value the kind that will stand
behind the action. Nothing that is
done for you is a matter of course.
Everything originates in a will for the
good, which is directed at you. Train
yourself never to put off the word
or action for the expression of
gratitude."

Albert Schweitzer

I saw the moon rise
I saw the sun set
Both at the same time.
Still there was a pause between them,
A breath.
What sits between these breaths?
I wondered.

My alarm went off at five a.m. I bundled myself up in my meditation shawl and wandered out into the chilly morning. The air felt fresh and crisp in my lungs. The silence of the street surrounded me with a calm stillness. I seemed to pause between each breath. The breeze was gentle against my face as I made my way with a few others to the Kumari Amman temple in Kanyakumari.

Kanyakumari is located at the very southern tip of India where the Indian Ocean meets the Bay of Bengal and the Arabian Sea. The Kumari Amman temple sits on this unusual land mass. It is a sight to behold.

As I continued my walk along a narrow passageway beside the temple, I turned a corner and came upon masses of Indians facing the east awaiting the rising of the sun. Some were making a pilgrimage from afar, and others lived in the area. My heart raced and then began to slow down. It appeared in this silence that surrounded me that there were many spaces between thoughts and breaths.

I carefully manoeuvred my way among the many people toward the ocean. There, in the water, I saw little boys frolicking and women wearing their colourful saris that gently floated with the movement of the sea, while others watched them come out of the water with their clothing hugging the contours of their bodies.

I felt as if I was witnessing stillness in motion while the sounds of the gentle morning wind permeated the air. Most of the people were facing east, but others mingled around the area waiting for the glorious sunrise. Some held their hands together in prayer position ("anjali mudra") at their heart, some held their right hand over their heart, while others had their arms at their sides, serenely looking off at the horizon.

They were here to welcome the Sun in the East,
And say goodnight to the Moon in the West.
They were Being Grateful for the Day to come,
As well as the Goodness and God within them.
They were Thanking each day with richness
To be alive, for yet another day.

It seemed so natural to begin the day in prayers and meditation that I wholeheartedly joined the crowd of worshippers in this celebration. As I continued my travels in India, I found this scene typically occurs at most sunrises and sunsets along the ocean. I somehow felt unusually at home in this situation. I felt joy and warmth rising inside of me. Then, I soon realized that this was just the beginning of the day.

One of the magical attributes of Kanyakumari is that you can see both the sun rising and the moon setting at the same time. The cycle of nature in each day is forever real. One end of the day hangs and pauses over the Bay of Bengal while the other travels over the confluence of the Indian Ocean and Arabian Sea.

In the early evening, this same scene is repeated, but this time looking to the west. Bus and carloads of people come from vast distances to this spiritual spot to bless the day and night. This time, though, a tremendous hubbub of activity was going on. There was food to celebrate; laughter and talking could be heard everywhere; vendors sold their commercial objects; and there were lots of playfulness as children played games and people went in and out the water.

In the evening, my travelling companion Jay and I were befriended by a group of young Indian guys who were interested in practicing their basic English with "the foreigners." We freely indulged their desire and chatted with them, learning more about their culture and life in India. They were so honest and I could feel them speak from their hearts.

The pride they felt in relating their realities and situations in life was profound to us. It was an eye opener to get a sense of what we consider in the West as naïveté. It was heartening to realize a pure view of life still exists, and I was reminded how jaded we have become in the West. Through this little celebration of gratitude to the sun and the moon, I realized that most Westerners have generally become so disconnected to the basics of nature and life. We have forgotten, if we ever knew, the space between the sun and the moon or the inhale and exhale of the breath.

The guys took us to the night lookout station where people can have a more powerful view. While we watched the sunset, they showed us to look in the opposite direction. What we saw shining brightly over the Bay of Bengal was the full opalescent beauty of the moon, her glorious warm glow welcoming the night and honouring her path. Ah, I felt the breathless pause. I felt such gratitude for this wonderful experience.

Twice a day this magnificent poetic reference to nature appears, when the moon goddess welcomes her mate, the sun, who then, in turn welcomes her. This relationship resides deep within us all. At the changeover from male to female and female to male, it is a time to realize we are both one—male and female, sun and moon, dwelling harmoniously within us at the same time. Nature speaks the truth so clearly and poignantly.

I began to wonder why we don't pay gratitude to the day in a similar, simple ceremony. I wondered how we do pay gratitude to our days, how we could become one with the day by practicing this little ceremony or something similar. When I returned to the West and my city life, I realized there definitely was a disconnection from the cycles of nature in my life. I just got back into my old habits and got bogged down with the functions of everyday life. Ah, where was the pause?

Yes, we have the choice of seeing our lives as just another day; we have to go to work, the arguments that will begin, or the children crying. Or we can move toward giving gratitude for our day in a positive way. We can use meditation, stillness, quiet moments, reading motivational and stimulating poetry, sayings, or literature, and many other techniques. We can even honour the sun by rising early to breathe in the radiance or the moon by gazing up to her as she disappears. Others may use prayer or repeat positive affirmations or mantras. There are many possibilities during our day to bless it, thanking it in our own ways. We can do this now, and it will make a difference in our state of being.

Indians and many other cultures for centuries have paid respect and gratitude to the day, and we can also learn from this practice. Can you imagine how grounded the setting of your day would be if you practiced being grateful for the day, everyone in it, and yourself? Put the beauty in your heart from the moment you wake. Then, remind yourself of this beauty at night as you wander into the dream state, and thank your day for being your special day.

Be grateful for your day.
Be grateful for other people's days.
Be grateful for the space between the sun
and the moon within you.
Be grateful for the day from your heart.
Be grateful for the pause between the breaths.
My wondering was over,
Because in the pause sits the true Self, You, God.

As we parted from the young men and they boarded the bus to return to their homes, I sensed that they had honoured us by showing us what life is like when it is lived from the heart. I learned to breathe a little bit more life this day. I learned to embrace the wisdom of simplicity, when nature is speaking to us.

Kanyakumari is truly a most amazing site to see. Find your own Kanyakumari experience and move into it from your heart. I am happy to have this simple, pure, and truthful memory. I can feel a smile coming on, a simple serene smile. Embrace the pause, when you will experience your true inner self. Be grateful.

DISCOVERY

What are you grateful for in life? ~ Have you ever stopped to think about gratitude and what it can do for you and others around you? ~ How does that make you feel? ~ Look for the treasure that appears before your eyes, as that is also a reflection of you.

6TH PEARL

Pearl • **Dreams**

Oyster • **Lisbon, Portugal**

*"Twenty
years from now you
will be more disappointed
by the things that you didn't
do than by the ones you did do.
So throw off the bowlines. Sail away
from the safe harbor. Catch the trade
winds in your sails. Explore. Dream.
Discover."*

MARK TWAIN

I was once standing at the Brussels airport en route to Lisbon for a weekend with my two roommates to celebrate the tenth anniversary of our acquaintance. As I waited to go through security, I noticed a billboard of a large red and white rocket ship. Written on it was a quote by Hergé (creator of *Tintin*) that read, "By believing in his dreams, a man turns them into reality." I was mesmerized by his words and wondered why it was so strategically placed in this area. Something about it affected me deeply. *Aha,* I thought, a pearl called "dreams."

When we arrived in Lisbon, we were tired from busy days at work but eager to discover this city that was the home of the great explorer Vasco da Gama. It was too early in the evening to go out on the town and partake in the nightlife, so we decided to take a "power nap," as we called them. As I lay in the dark, eyes open, with flashing lights from the street reflecting in my window, I found my mind wandering back to the billboard I had seen just a few hours before.

I pondered the nature of my own dreams, and began to reflect upon those times in my life when my dreams actually had become reality.

I remembered watching a television program when I was perhaps nine or ten years old. A man on the show was talking about dreams. He encouraged his audience to write a dream list of all the things, places, and activities that you would like to possess or accomplish in life. He then said to put this list away in a safe place and from time to time take it out and reflect upon it.

As a young boy, I was truly excited by the prospect of undertaking this new activity. After the show was over, I promptly went to my bedroom and began dreaming. I began to record my aspirations on a little piece of paper—things I wanted to achieve, to own, to discover in my life.

When we are young, everything seems to be within the realm of possibility—the world is, so to speak, our oyster. After listening to the man, I somehow realized that if I was to accomplish anything in my life, I needed to actively envision my goals and aspirations.

I finished my dream list and then promptly put it in a safe place. Well, I didn't find it again for years—not an unfamiliar occurrence for most people. What I understand now is that this action was instilling my dreams into my cells, neurons, and my whole body, in both conscious and unconscious form. The act of writing my dreams down and keeping them safe was also sending them into the universe and trusting that whatever was to come forth in future was very important, and perhaps even necessary, for my development. I was creating my destiny. I was letting the universe have its say.

About twenty years later as I was rummaging through my mother's house, I miraculously found this little piece of paper with my dream list. I took some time to sit down, read, and reflect upon it. It was astonishing what I had learned from this dream list I had created many years before.

To my amazement, I have accomplished many of the items on that list. Some in full, some in part, but most have manifested themselves in some way in my life. Some of the items on the list were becoming a national champion figure skater and a contemporary dancer; obtaining a university degree; and travelling to Egypt and other countries, including Thailand because the physical beauty of their Miss Universe winner mesmerized me. I had totally forgotten all of the things I had put on the list. Now I was receiving the gift of this simple exercise; it really did work.

Once I had read the list, I decided to again put it in another safe place. Not surprisingly, that safe place is again forgotten and I now often wonder what became of that piece of paper. Is it somewhere still in my mother's house or has it been thrown away? I hope that I find the list again one day, as I would like to frame it. This was my first recollection of dreams, how to invent them and then proceed to create them. My life today is a result of many of the items written down on that list. I am amazed at the power of intention and the choices I made over many years to make those early dreams reality.

"By believing in his dreams, man turns them into reality." Reflecting upon the Hergé's quote led me to remember other dreams that have turned into reality in their own way.

I once wanted to be a world champion figure skater, but I didn't achieve this in the way I originally wished. Instead, I ended up choreographing the winning championship performances of one of the world's greatest skaters, which was an amazing experience. And, my dream to compete at the Olympics came true in a different way, by directing and choreographing the closing ceremonies of the 1988 Calgary Winter Olympics. I even dreamed of writing a book one day. I have also dreamed of having a sacred space to which I can always return; this has become a journey along a lifelong path and has been drawing nearer as time goes on.

As I continued to lie there, many more dreams flashed by in my mind. It was a tremendously colourful and light-driven journey. I began to integrate the meaning of Hergé's quote with my reality. The feeling was amazing. I somehow never gave myself credit for believing in these dreams and what has manifested by simply allowing myself to have them.

I have come to learn that dreams appear in your mind as well as your body, heart, and soul. They most likely start from a deep internal desire. They are fantastic sources for visualization. Dreams inspire us in so many ways, and when uttered internally the senses get involved. We can see, feel, touch, taste, and smell them. Once we sense them wholly, dreams then come deeply from the heart and are connected to our values, and become more real.

Honestly believe in your dreams. Have passion for your dreams. Just ask for them, believe in them, and be ready to receive in the form they are to be given to you.

We don't have to be kids to dream. Dreaming is an integral part of life and should never end until we are off into the ether. They are part of our survival and hope in this world. But remember, with dreams, some may take more energy and determination than others, and some may not turn out to be exactly how you first envisioned them, but once you put energy, focus, and determination behind them, watch out—energy follows attention.

I have made new dreams lists since my first one, as well as lists of goals and outcomes to help me attain the items on the list. Sometimes when we start with a goal or an outcome in mind it can simply be accomplished methodically as we move toward the finish line. So you may want to dream first then create goals and outcomes to attain them.

I have learned by this reflection, dreams often have their own time frame and you simply can't rush them. They will happen when the time is absolutely right. There is also a very strong sense of "surrender" to them.

We all have dreams, so many dreams. Put a heartfelt, passionate intention behind your dreams and see what can happen. Set them into action; apply focus and effort with a dash of intensity and energy. But also allow them to have flow and freedom. However, mostly dream, as this is where life all begins. Manifest your heartfelt dreams, and if they don't happen, do not fret because it may come in a different form or way than you ever expected. The ones that do come true are the ones that are right for you. Keep moving toward them. *Aha*, set them free.

Later, I arose from my power nap and went into the Lisbon night, full of buoyancy at the realization that I can make more of my dreams come true, if I really want to. A dream I had focused on but a month before this trip was to fall in love again; I hadn't been in love for such a long time. And I dreamed just that on that fine Lisbon weekend. I sailed like Vasco da Gama over the seven seas. Another dream was coming true.

When I returned to Brussels, I took a moment to stop and look back at the billboard again. I said to myself, "I really wonder how many people have actually registered this quote or have even seen it?" I smiled and thought yes, this quote is truth. I listened to the quote and will continue to do so. It has given me such insight and wisdom.

I am glad I watched that television show, believed in what was said, and then, took action to creating a new reality.

"By believing in his dreams, a man turns them into reality."

Dare to dream, friends, make them your reality. Celebrate the realization of your dreams!

DISCOVERY

Do you believe in dreams? ~ What dreams have become realities in one way or another? ~ Take a moment to celebrate them with gratitude, as you have created those dreams and your destiny. Allow yourself to set your sails and discover the world of dreams. Make them a reality with just enough energy. What are you dreams now? ~ Follow that energy of attention toward the dream. How do you feel now?

7TH PEARL

Pearl • **Presence**

Oyster • **Puerto Vallarta, Mexico**

*"You
can become
blind by seeing each
day as a similar one. Each
day is different one, each day
brings a miracle of its own. It's
just a matter of paying attention to
this miracle."*

PAULO COELHO

The waves pounded against the sandy beach. The sun shone down brightly, making the surface of the dark blue ocean dance with diamonds. People from all over the world frolicked in the sea, dodging the large waves, riding the smaller waves, body surfing, swimming farther out in the ocean to avoid the rollers, and parachuting high above the ocean. They were laughing, talking, smiling, tanning their bodies, drinking piña coladas, and devouring delicious Mexican food. Local merchants strolled about selling trinkets, carpets, jewellery, hats, and other souvenirs. It was a glorious mixture of humanity. People living for the moment, present in the moment.

Have you ever wondered about being present? What it would be like for you?

I experienced that same beach scene everyday during my stay in Puerto Vallarta. Time felt like it hung there in the moment. Everyone seemed to be present in the now, living the experience. I, too, was living it.

My day began by rising early to eat my breakfast while I awaited the sun to raise its glowing face above the hill behind my hotel. As the sun peeked its face forth, more and more joy rose in my body and heart. I could sense pulsations throughout my whole being. As the sun rose, I felt it rising inside of me and I cherished its presence.

If you blink you will miss it.
It will
never
reappear,
at least
not
in the same
moment,

time,
and
space.
Presence is here, now.

I finished my breakfast and headed out onto the streets as the world woke up. The shops slowly opened, people wandered around as they looked for a restaurant, and some early birds went to the beach to take up residence for the day. I wandered to the Cybersmoothie Café to check my email and write. I was working on the second draft of my book. I drank a delicious smoothie as I wrote. Time seemed to be hanging, millisecond by millisecond. It was inspiring to be present with my writing and my surroundings.

After a couple of hours, I returned to my room and prepare for the afternoon of tanning on the beach. It seemed and felt as if every step I took back to my room was forever placed with presence. The cobblestones on the roads made walking a challenge because of my choice of footwear. The sidewalks went up and down, and if I wasn't careful I could go flying at any moment. I definitely needed to be present for this. I smiled at tourists who passed by, saying hello or "hola." The brightly coloured flowers that hung over the walls and buildings were a sight to behold. Inside of me, I felt I was there, completely there, without wavering. The sense of presence was powerful indeed.

I say presence,
the ever-present now.
Blink and you may have missed
the opportunity of your life.

Be on guard always,
Be alert
for presence,
and engage with all your heart now.

My afternoons were spent, as they often were, lounging on the beach. I met new friends and watched the many people. It is so wonderful to observe people and their actions. I asked myself, Are they aware of the presence they are in? They certainly seemed to me to be in the present and in the now, but were they? What will happen to them when they return home?

Late in the afternoon as the sun began to wane, I left the beach and went back to my hotel to shower and remove all that sand as well as the tanning lotion that blessed my pores. Following that, I lathered my skin with lovely cream to keep the skin moistened and refreshed. This presence was a very sensual moment in time.

I headed back to Cybersmoothie to be present again with my writing. The walk was always fascinating as tanned regulars and burned newcomers were now moving from beach mode to the happy-hour mode. Occasionally, I would drop into a grocery shop and buy a few items and have a little chat in Spanish with the shopkeeper.

As I wrote my stories, I found I became perfectly aligned and present with my past. In other words, my past was now being re-created in the present, re-lived in the present through writing and tied to the future with the goal that people would be reading them. The past, present, and future are interconnected in many ways. Staying in the present tends to ground, centre, and focus you.

After finishing my writing, I returned to the hotel to dress for dinner. On the way back to the hotel, I practiced being present.

Presence,
taking the time to be present,
spending my energy in the present.

One day as I sat eating dinner with new found friends, I had a moment in between conversations and I thought,

Energy is not equal to time,
how do you spend energy to be present?
Not tomorrow,
not yesterday,
but now.
For all you have is your presence,
what you had, is yesterday,
is a memory today.
What you have tomorrow
is a thought for tomorrow
it is not now.
It is important to savour
and
relish
the presence
for this is
our existence
now
and forevermore
because tomorrow,
the next millisecond,

the next second,
the next minute,
may never appear,
so stay present forevermore.

The days passed like this, save variations in whom I met, dined, with or spoke to. One evening I went to dinner with a Mexican artist who seemed to be wearing a rather troubled energy. His face showed this and hence the rest of his body. I asked him what are his dreams for this new year. He said, "I want to be more engaged with people on a deeper level." My reply to him was, "I like to practice being in the now, being present." He replied, "How can you only live in the now and not think about the future, your goals?"

I thought about this for a moment, then I said, "To me, being in the now is about being present, engaged, fully here." I explained that I do believe in the future and that it is important to make goals. But to me, having presence means to be aware of all aspects of life; for example, being present with him now, listening to him, and seeing him fully. It is the same when I am walking down the street; to be present with my steps, the environment, people, and even with writing my book at Cybersmoothie. I also mentioned to him that I sometimes find myself not in the present, and that it takes practice, conscious practice, until it becomes habit, to be present.

Living with presence does not mean being devoid of future thoughts. It is being present with those particular thoughts at that moment in time while being stationed, fully engaged, in the now. When a person lives in the future they rarely can appreciate the glory of what is being presented to them now. They lose track of their immediate senses, become distant or disconnected with their environments. Bring your future thoughts to be fully engaged in the present, and be one with them, now. Put your energy here, in the present; this will propel you to the future when it arrives.

Every step I take is now,
it is the present.
As I stand on the corner watching the cars go by,
this is presence.
I am here in the present,
Now.
Or,
as I sit, engaged in a conversation
with you, with many others,
I am there in fullness,
I am present.
Or,
as I watch the leaves fall gracefully
to the ground in autumn,
being present with them
is being alive and engaged.
Or,
when I put my mind to a goal,
I focus, then visualize it,
but keep my feet grounded in the present
as that is where the learning for the future is,
The Present.

My friend said to me, "It is wonderful that you can be this way." He also said he struggled with this way of being, as do many of us. We can all have and live a life of presence. It simply takes practice.

Presence is also about being
fully happy with ourselves,
so that
we stay centered in our body.
You sense in your body
the feeling
of being placed
in the present,
engaged, fully engaged.
Sense in your body
the place
of presence.

As we parted company that night and I felt present with him, I sensed an uncomfortable uneasiness surrounding his soul.

Once
you have said
Now,
that Now no longer exists,
another presence appears
and when
it is gone,
vanished

into time immemorial,
it is now history.
As these words flow out of my hand
they become history
and
memories
of things that were.
Time that was,
can be remembered by living presence.
Life is forever
shifting,
changing,
transforming,
into new perspectives,
thoughts, ideas,
and we can move with it,
live it,
or we can reject it.
It is our choice.
Search inside of yourself
and then be one
with presence,
now.

I sat on the beach watching the last sunset of my stay in Puerto Vallarta with a friend. I gazed toward the sun and watched it slide down over the edge of the horizon. Moments later, the sky began to change colours, turning into radiant degrees of oranges and yellows. Presence in time, energy, and space flowed like the ocean with each millisecond.

As darkness prevailed, the stars appeared like diamonds, the moon was bright and music wafted through the air as party time had begun.

The memories of my vacation are so vivid in my mind, body, and soul. I shall remember that I was conscious of presence in Puerto Vallarta. I practiced it every day with mindfulness. It was something that flowed through me and also seemed to flow through many whom I encountered and observed. Create a present state of being, as this is packed with incredible energy that will motivate and inspire you forever.

Returning home from Puerto Vallarta I thought, How can I do this when I am back in my busy life? This is the challenge for all of us in modern day society. But being present is not far from our reach. It is really about being aware of what is important to your state of happiness and then living it. All is possible. Once you have tasted presence, you want more. It is a state of mind, a state of presence.

Live with presence right now, wherever you are and whatever you are doing. That is when the magic of life is revealed at it fullest.

DISCOVERY

What does living in the present mean for you? ~ Have you ever given it some thought? ~ How do you live in the present? ~ Are you present now? ~ If so, what is different for you now compared to when you are not being present? ~ Consider the space between your breaths; breathe and reflect. Take the time to engage, now, and sense what it does for your performance in life.

Pearl • **Sense**

Oyster • **San Marcos, USA**

*"All
our knowledge
has it foundations in the
senses."*

LEONARDO DA VINCI

I was visiting San Marcos, a sleepy town north of San Diego, California that at first glance appears to be a pensioner's paradise. On my first afternoon there, I ate lunch at a golf club, watching the elderly practice their swings, tee off, and play a hole. I looked around in the restaurant and realized that I was many years younger than the rest of the clientele. Feeling slightly uncomfortable, the question popped into my mind, "Will this be me in a few more years? Do I need to learn to play golf now?"

I was visiting San Marcos attending a two-week training camp to study trance and learn to put people into trance for therapeutic purposes. Trance is "a naturalistic learning state which is supported by the ritualistic experience of hypnotherapy." As the training progressed, it seemed as if I was put into trance everyday by osmosis, from the teacher's gentle voice. I must admit that I was experiencing some profound realizations during the training. Many of them appeared after I left San Marcos, when the unconsciousness residue of the studies began to take effect, but one realization appeared to me on the last day of the trance camp.

I was sitting in a lovely little diner that was again frequented by many seniors. Waitresses wore red shorts, white blouses, and many had big hairdos. Most of them worked very fast and generally exhibited that good old American hospitality and smiles. I had just ordered my traditional two eggs over easy with brown toast and hash browns.

Along came a fellow camp participant whom I had wanted to have a conversation with since I first saw him earlier that week. He joined me for breakfast. We began talking about our lives, trance camp, and what was coming up for us in the next while. I began to speak about a relationship with a friend that had been concerning me.

This friend often spoke to me as if he were my father. He seemed often embarrassed of me and sometimes condescending. I felt as though I was going into an unwanted trance when this would happen. I had basically had enough of our relationship.

My breakfast companion said it appeared I was not being seen, heard, or felt. I don't know what happened at that point, but I felt an explosive realization happen inside of me. *Aha*, not being "sensed."

The man at the breakfast table said, "Do you want others to see, hear, and feel you for your thoughts, your ways, and who you are?"

Yes, I thought, that's it. What a revelation. I guess it took the many trances I experienced at the training to jolt this awareness from my unconscious.

I began immediately to wonder about his observation and was so excited it was as if I had found a new toy to play with. As I ate my eggs and hash browns, I thought, often in communication this is the missing link, the gap between myself and my friends, family, and the many acquaintances I have in life. Isn't this what my friend and I were doing—communicating, but not fully communicating with our senses? Perhaps we were communicating with our senses, but only through our own eyes, our own scripts of the world and then blindly not sensing the other person.

As our breakfast continued, my thoughts led me to think about Gandhi's principles of non-violence for change and transformation. The word violence comes from the verb "to violate." When I consider this way of being, I realized that the conflicts and disagreements with my friend were coming at me as a violation of who I am, my identity, my being. When we would have these rare moments, his physical presence would overwhelm me like a wild animal. I felt I couldn't escape and his eyes would become very large and frightening to me. I was feeling violated.

As my classmate and I continued to chat about this concept, this new awareness profoundly strengthened my will to sense the effects of conversations and situations I get myself involved with.

I was eager to engage my friend back home in what I was learning. My relationship with him was too important for me to simply throw it away.

With this knowledge, I wanted to invite him to sense my realization: to see, hear, or feel someone, something, or some situation is about being present and to be involved unconditionally. No walls, no agendas. It is about giving your energy to them without losing your centre, and being actively engaged in supporting this person, thing, or situation. Once we get ourselves out of the way of our own agenda, ego, and rigid thoughts, we can be flexible and empathize with others. This is the space where a fruitful conversation and solutions can then take place.

I eventually had this conversation with my friend and he listened to my concerns. I told him how I felt violated in our friendship and I was wondering why we even liked each other let alone have a love for each other. I approached this subject in a very supportive way. We both felt safe. He apologized, and told me to tell him when his words or actions made me feel violated, as he sometimes isn't conscious of when he is doing this. After this conversation, he later wrote me an email saying that he realized some of our conflicts we spoke of have been based on the fact that he has tried to make me live by his script, "but that is impossible to do," he said.

Living according to someone else's script or plan is not possible for any of us to do. When having such expectations of others, we need to consider if we are violating their being. When we truly sense someone, then we are on the road to greater presence and winning solutions. This is power in itself and can lead to a higher level of awareness and stronger relationships.

Since that insight I have been practicing seeing, hearing, and feeling others, situations, and the environment with more conscious action. It is also about the reflection of honouring and seeing myself at the same time. The trick is to stay centred on who you sense you are, with flexibility, and then expand your concept of yourself to embrace others by sensing them for who they are. There was one point during a period of conflict with my friend I decided to expand my learning and embrace the situation by make an intensive choice to suggest that we consult a mediator. My friend jumped at this idea, agreeing immediately, and after our session with the mediator, our relationship quickly improved. The spell was finally broken.

Helen Keller once said, “The most pathetic person in the world is someone who has sight but no vision.” This quote can be applied to this pearl. When you go into your next conversation with another person, see him or her with an open mind, vision, and sense so that you are not violating that person or yourself. Become one with them, be supportive in a learning manner, and simply get out of the way of the oncoming traffic—the traffic in your own head, your agenda, your script.

The result of my conversation with my friend has taken us to a new level of respect and honour for each other. We are committed to taking little steps toward making changes in the way we understand each other.

I now practice seeing, feeling, and healing with consciousness and clarity. I have realized that everyone wants to be heard, seen, and felt. We want to be sensed. It is amazing how this knowledge has transformed the courage in myself, in the risks I take, and in my conversations. I am simply happier for this pearl.

Also, I now realize that when I arrived in San Marcos, I was not sensing this retirement village for really what it was before making my judgment. As I looked around the restaurant full of retirees, I could now see, feel, and hear San Marcos and retirement with a completely different vision. I feel more flexible in my mind, more present, and I realized this scene would include me in not so many years to come. How wonderful is it to live a slower lifestyle, remain very active, and enjoy the sun each day?

Sense now. It is a two-way street.

DISCOVERY

How do you sense the world around you? ~ How do you sense others? ~ Is the script of your mind not allowing you to see, feel, or hear others as well as yourself with an open mind? ~ Take a step back and look at how you communicate. What do you see now? ~ Be honest and clear about your vision.

Pearl • **Trust**

Oyster • **Vancouver, Canada**

"When
a person really
desires something, all the
universe conspires to help that
person realize his dream."

PAULO COELHO

Trust. I have come to believe that to be able to truly trust may be one of the biggest challenges I've faced in my life. I had struggled with this vast concept continuously for many years until I decided to truly make an effort to understand how trust manifests itself in life.

In 2001, I had the opportunity to direct a large and challenging project, the opening and closing ceremonies of the 8th IAAF World Championships in Athletics in Edmonton. After taking a few months off to recover from the job, I decided to spend three weeks at a meditation and yoga retreat in Ganeshpuri, India.

After spending my days in meditation, silence, chanting, and reading, I left the ashram in a state of bliss. I could not have been in a more open and receptive state of being. I felt as though the world was new and I was observing and experiencing it through a new pair of glasses.

After leaving the ashram, I intuited that something much bigger was beginning to happen inside of me. I could not put my finger on what it was at all. I just knew I felt fresh, new. Nevertheless, it was also uncomfortable and I felt at times as if I was living in two parallel universes; one was the spiritual inner world and the other was the practical, professional, everyday world.

On my arrival home, I began to look for work again. I thought how great it would be to have a new project refresh, invigorate, and excite me. No work opportunities had come out of the last project; in fact, absolutely no job prospects were on the horizon and I wondered what I was going to do. What was happening to my professional universe?

I made all my usual contacts in the skating, live event, and film worlds, but I kept hitting dead ends. It was so bizarre and I couldn't remember a time like this before in my life. I sensed frustration mounting and a bit of panic seemed to be setting in. My blissful state was evaporating and my savings were diminishing.

During this time I had been corresponding with my roommate from

Ganeshpuri and I told him about my situation. He wrote some interesting thoughts to me:

"Use this precious time wisely and learn from your experiences in India. Listen to what was being spoken to you. Listen to your inner Guru. Allow the expansion of your blissful state to see new horizons. Be wise and trust in the message(s) you are being given. We are rarely in life given this gift of time in life to do this reflection and move within. Trust and when it seems that you are losing the power of trust, go deeper inside and trust more. You will be supported."

Well, I was definitely receiving a message. I listened to the words from my roommate and really sensed deep inside he was right. This was the spiritual universe speaking loudly. Everyday, I began to visualize, set intentions, and meditate on trust, and when doubt appeared with its uncomfortable face, I would again believe in trust.

At this point, with some deep contemplation, I decided to devote my energies toward the film business for one year. I wanted to discover it and find out if it truly would be the business of my passions.

The first success of this intention arrived: I received a grant to produce and shoot a short dance film. It was a wonderful experience and I felt supported by so many people in the business. The film was a success. A year after it was made, it was accepted by film festivals, bought by TV stations from around the world, and garnered two British Columbia Leo Film Awards for Editing and Direction. I thought, Wow, there must be support for me in the film industry.

I then partnered up with a few producer friends and we worked to create other film projects. Together, we created concept after concept. One reached development stage and others simply could not find funding nor interest. I was beginning to sense that film was a tough, very tough business in which to make a living. My trust was declining on this front, but on a spiritual front, I was beginning to experience the fruit of my efforts.

During that year, everywhere I turned it seemed a film grant or development money would appear to help me through the tough times. Each day, I continued to believe in trust. Trust. It was my mantra. I was coming back to what my roommate in India had talked about. I trusted that everything would work out.

As this was happening, I was feeling that some real changes were happening to me spiritually and in the way I was observing and responding to life. I could also sense inside of me that something was telling me to leave Vancouver for a while. It was a rather uneasy voice that was speaking to me. I wasn't sure if I should listen or not. I didn't want to make a mistake. I was uncertain of where I was being led. I thought, how can I make a move when there is not much money in my accounts, no concrete future possibilities, and when my mother is at her advanced age? Trust, I kept saying to myself, something will come about.

Money was becoming more of an issue, but it still kept appearing and in the right amount I would ask for. No less and no more. My financial state was a message telling me to trust; this is only what I needed and it is the right amount to support me. Trust.

In a location away from Vancouver. I was setting this desire into action. I sent it into the universe. One thing led to the next. I sensed an increased momentum, that something was definitely about to happen. But what, where, how, and when was I about to experience?

I got an invitation to present my latest short dance film at an international dance film conference in Monte Carlo. I attended the conference and also spent time visiting friends in Paris, Brussels, and Amsterdam. My search for my new destination ended in Brussels when my friend Robin said, "Why don't you come and live here for six months? You can stay for free as it would be great to work on developing a production together. Besides, it would be great to have you living close by." I had never thought of living in Brussels. Was this the shift that was happening inside of me?

After some contemplation of family and business matters, I decided to definitely make the move. I would be starting all over again, from nothing and no income—again! But I was again being supported and I trusted, no matter how risky the move may have seemed. I never turned back on this decision, even with many naysayers advising me otherwise.

While in Canada gathering my things together, I was given another opportunity: a grant to go back to Europe for dance film festival in Barcelona and a conference in London. I returned to Brussels and invited my good friend Bojan from Amsterdam to visit me.

My life remained vibrant by trusting that all would be fine and work out. I was not living off of my abundant bank account of the past, but I was still living my life in a similar fashion with just enough money—and always with trust on my side. As I welcomed trust in my life, I sensed my universes were coming closer and closer together.

In Brussels, I began to reinvent my life. A few weeks into my new life in Belgium, I made the decision to spend my fiftieth birthday in India. I was about to write to a friend in India to tell him of my plans when another friend emailed me exactly at the same moment asking if I wanted to go to India with him on a business class flight, for free. I couldn't believe what I was reading. Trust.

Following this, a friend asked me to design her wedding in Spain—a first for me. While I was there, I met a wonderful woman who was to become my personal coach. Trust. At the end of my coaching sessions with her, I decided that the film business was not for me, but personal and executive coaching was what I wanted to do with my life. Trust.

Then within a few months of arriving in Brussels, Bojan began a relationship with Robin and he moved from Amsterdam to live with us. Trust.

So many wonderful situations occurred in those two years, during my discovery and practicing of trust. I could feel my universes powerfully coming together, with each one supporting the other. I never, in this whole period, thought I would end up on the street or starving or without ambition or support from friends, family, or financial sources. I trusted that all would work out, with the kindness and support from everyone around me. When one situation ended and I thought, Oh now the end is near, what will I do? Another situation appeared that supported my belief in trust. My international life of travelling never stopped during this whole time, which was totally incredible to me. In fact, my travelling increased. My life just became more vibrant and full. How I got the money is beyond me, but I was supported.

Every person's life is different and one may say I am lucky. Perhaps so, but when we are in the thick of change or hardship and we don't see the luck at all we still have a choice to trust. I had the choice to go into a downward spiral and sink myself into "poor me" thinking and victimization or I could choose to look up, toward possibilities, hope, and learning. I chose the upward spiral, even if it did not always seem to be moving upward. I trusted and still do, more than ever, know that all will work out in the end.

My journey continues: finances have improved dramatically; my travel continues to increase; my life continues to expand intellectually and spiritually; my trust just continues to grow and grow. I do realize one thing, though, there is a key to trusting. We need to believe that all will work out the best possible way no matter how difficult it can be. We need to support our belief with positive effort and action toward where we want to go; even if we may or may not know the direction, it is guaranteed to change along the way. It is about trusting we will make the right choices, and if they are not, they will become learning experiences, moving us forward in our journey toward trust and trusting the universes that exist within and outside of us. This is the bigger picture in life.

My roommate in Ganeshpuri was correct. "You are being given this time to sort out some things in life." Trust. Trust. Trust. That inner voice of trust is unflinching now and has a steadfast beat within me.

Open your heart to trust.
Open your heart to put the effort in.
Open your heart so that trust can flow through it.
Open the dam to let trust flow like
a river toward the ocean.
Your heart is what holds your power to trust.

DISCOVERY

What is your relationship with trust now? ~ What do you trust in life? ~ What can stop you from trusting in life? ~ Take a few moments to reflect upon what trust means to you and recognize the situations in your life when you trusted and when you didn't. Are there differences? ~ What would they be? ~ Open your heart to trusting now and experience the bliss of where this can lead you in life.

Pearl • **Honour**

Oyster • **Victoria, Canada**

"The shortest and surest way to live with honour in the world is to be in reality what we would appear to be; all human virtues increase and strengthen themselves by the practice and experience of them."

SOCRATES

There are many places and times in life when one experiences honour. Honour lives inside of our cells and souls. It's deeply rooted in us, sometimes so strongly that it can hold us back. Family, friends, our environment, cultural traditions, and much more create this unconscious value, which can be likened to roots holding our feet to the earth.

I have experienced honour many times in my life, but one experience in particular remains profound and forever interwoven with my heart.

One autumn day, I was walking on the tree-lined street in Victoria, Canada, where I grew up. The brilliant and rich colours of autumn foliage surrounded me. Suddenly, a lightning bolt went off inside, and a vision appeared before me in my mind. Dumbfounded, I stopped walking. I looked around and found no one was on the street. Immersed in my vision, my body turned to light and I felt lightness and smiles spread through like blood rushing from my heart.

A bit of background is in order, as this vision had a definite genesis, beginning with my fiftieth birthday.

I had recently moved to Brussels and I decided to celebrate the landmark in India, but before arriving there, I went on my own world birthday party tour to reflect the gypsy-like and whimsical nature of my extraordinary life journey. The first party would be at my new home Brussels. My roommates threw a glorious bash for me. The multi-levelled, art deco home was filled with people, many of whom were new acquaintances and friends of my roommates. This party represented a new decade, a new era, a new beginning for me.

It was also a fabulous bash because four long-time friends from London, Toronto, and Switzerland attended. The weekend with them was so full of laughter, love, and happiness. We reminisced over and over again. I can't remember a time filled with such frivolity and silliness. The laughter that resonated in the air was directly coming from our hearts. Truth was embodied in these full joyous sounds.

Then, a few days later, I got on a plane and travelled to Vancouver for two more celebratory parties in my honour. One was a small dinner party in a fine restaurant with some extremely close friends. The other party, held by my former roommates had an Indian theme, due to my love for India and the upcoming trip there. It was comprised of old friends from my skating and film days plus other walks of life. All ages were gloriously represented and my mother even made the trip from Victoria to attend this incredible bash.

Continuing along on my fiftieth birthday tour, I went to Victoria where my sister had arranged a delightful party with family, old friends from elementary school to university, and my oldest friend of all, Jeanette, whom I had known since infancy. I had now attended four parties in three cities, two countries, and two continents, representing my exciting history, incredible relationships and rewarding accomplishments. How gratifying and fascinating that was to me. I felt very thankful indeed for these gifts in my life.

On that autumn day in Victoria, as I stood on the street of my youth, my vision was so profound. I was standing on the top of a mountain. I looked down and saw the different paths of my life. Some were well traveled and some not so well traveled; some short and others very long. They curved and intersected and then curved some more. Never a straight line. I scanned them with bewilderment. What I saw standing at different points along the paths were many different pillars. The pillars represented the people in my life.

I looked down at each one of the pillars, contemplating their relationship to me. I saw big smiling pillars. I saw pillars of strength. I saw pillars of all ages standing with tenderness, fierceness, and playfulness. There were so many different pillars, dead and alive.

I remember then turning and looking up and seeing another mountain to climb, it was high and steep with snow on the top of it. I turned to my pillars of strength, my friends, and I said, "Follow me, we aren't done yet."

We then began our climb upward, with more wisdom, toward the next half century of my life.

This was such an honour for me to realize that these important people have been long time friends, have been colleagues who followed my career in silence or exuberance, or have been acquaintances who I have seen only a few times in so many years without much correspondence. I realized this is what life is about. There is nothing more amazing in life than family and friends. All the rest is camouflage. The rest is just a façade for the real thing, family and friends. They make up the total of one's life; they are the salt of the earth; and they are the roots that ground you to the earth.

It all comes down to one thing, the honour to love these people who have supported and cheered me throughout life. I am thankful for their gifts of just being there, close or far away in space or in mind.

Of course we are not happy with everyone all the time and as time goes by the pillars may disappear or collapse. Those are the paths on the mountain that end for whatever reason, but they were all important for the journey. The ones that remain in your life, till the very end, are those that, on the many different levels, fit with your spirit. I am honoured to still have my old friends and honoured when I have new friends who become another pillar on my path.

I may not be saying anything new or perhaps, I regard this with a little naïveté. However, we often don't fully see the spectrum of this honour, this gift, this universal truth in our lives.

I am honoured by many other situations, projects, and gifts in life. This comes from a special place inside of each of us. It is called the heart. That is where love sits. That is where honour is received and felt. It is full of spirit. It is full of calmness and humility. It is a cup which is filled to the brim and flowing over.

Finally, my tour would end in Ottawa where I would meet with more old friends. It was fantastic. They were so happy that I had finally reached fifty. These friends were older than me and I could see that these very bright and adventurous people had now made new lives for themselves after retiring. Their energies were vibrant, healthy, and most of all playful. If I doubted life after fifty, they elegantly displayed that I can definitely live a very powerful life way after fifty. This was magical realization for me.

Honour yourself by honouring others.

It is an honour to be alive,
a true gift.
Honour's home is within
the heart.
Everyone has different situations
in life where
honour can be
realized,
sensed,
and represented.
It is there within you and
happening all the time.
Let it blossom forth
to
its
deserved
magnificence.

DISCOVERY

Take a look at what you honour in your life and ask, does it come from your heart? ~ What is your relationship with honour in your life? ~ What do you honour? ~ What does this give to you when you sense its incredible value? ~ How do you express honour? ~ Spend some moments now reflecting on how honour resonates in your life.

Pearl • **Freedom**

Oyster • **Petra, Jordan**

"Between
stimulus and
response, there is a space.
In that space, lies our freedom
and power to choose our response.
In our response, lies our growth and
freedom."

VICTOR FRANKL

Strong as the Desert
Move as the Wind
Soft as the Sand
Forever Free.
—Kahlid Aoud Al. Bdoll

One very hot day in May, I found myself sitting in an ancient amphitheatre in Petra, Jordan. It was late in the afternoon and the sun was beginning to descend, leaving a variety of shadows and an intense, ever-changing rose colour on the surrounding hills, cave entrances, and decaying historic buildings for my keen eye to absorb. It was definitely a sight to behold and cherish.

Most tourists had left the archaeological site, leaving the Bedouins to freely frolic around. It was as if now, in the freedom of nature, their home Petra was returned to them. Children were on donkeys, some were on horses, and others ran around in their Bedouin and Western garb, enjoying the late afternoon sun.

As I sat in the amphitheatre, the sounds of people chatting and laughing floated in the air. Off in the distance, I heard the sweet music of an instrument playing. I looked up to the top of the amphitheatre and saw two men sitting side by side. One was playing a lute. The delicious, delicate music was as sweet as sugar. It sounded divine in this very romantic and ancient setting. The sense of freedom and peacefulness blissfully embraced me.

I waved to the men in a friendly gesture. They waved back, and proceeded to walk to where I was sitting. They sat down with me and we struck up a conversation. I watched their every gesture with intrigue. They were very humourous, these early twenty- something Bedouin men dressed in Western clothes, holding mobile phones in their hands, and wearing rings on all their fingers and bandannas around their heads. It was as if they were enjoying their Western look but mocking it at the same time. It was very amusing to me. I sensed their inner soulful freedom from their body language and facial expressions.

One of the pair, Kahlid, was really chatty, the other totally quiet. He told me he had visited Europe. He said Western society was laughable to him with its crazy and mad lifestyles and emphasis on material possessions. "Why do they make things so complicated?" he said. "One needs very little to survive in life—food, clothes, roof over your head, perhaps, a little money, and love." He observed that we were prisoners of our own freedom. He said, "Look around you at this place full of beauty, strength, power, spirit, and most of all, freedom."

Then he turned away with his glassy eyes looking out over ancient Petra and the following words flowed out of his soul,

Strong as the Desert
Move as the Wind
Soft as the Sand
Forever Free.

He said that the spirit of Bedouins is reflected in those words. These elegant words resounded within me with the force of nature in which they were given to me. The essence of the Bedouins is freedom of movement in space, mind, body, and soul. Nomadic in nature, they roam the land, just as their contemporary mobile phones roam for a connection.

The freedom I sensed from Kahlid and his understanding of life was that of a wise old man. It was very simple. Nature for him was where freedom existed. I sensed that this was the same for all Bedouins.

I wondered if the other tourists reflected on this pearl of freedom while they experienced Petra. What was going through the tourists' minds? Where was their Bedouin nature? Where was my Bedouin nature?

This Bedouin nature for me began earlier in the day. It started by a horseback ride to the entry of the Siq. My memory flashed back to the movie Indiana Jones and the Last Crusade, which had inspired my trip to Petra. In the movie, Indiana Jones also rode horseback into this majestic and mysterious world. I had tingles up my spine, realizing my visit to Petra was fulfilling a dream.

The Siq is a long and windy ravine leading to ancient Petra. "Where am I heading?" I thought. I felt so tiny as my eyes followed the gently carved rock face up to the top of the ravine. My mind wandered, wondering how many centuries of people walked or ran or rode horses down this ravine. What could have happened here? If only the rocks could speak.

The smooth and textured rock face around and above me changed continually. The sun's shadows created various patterns on the shapes, drawing out the different colours within the stone. Often, I saw the image of an elephant or of two faces looking at each other. At one point, the shadows on the ground reminded me of a river flowing to the ocean.

I continued to walk freely flowing down the Siq river to the metaphoric ocean, when all of a sudden there is was before me. The majestic, pink stone "Treasury" building, where Indian Jones entered, stood in front of me, carved into the rock face of the Siq. The tall pillars of the Treasury graced its entrance dwarfed the people surrounding it. Its grandeur and unusual pink colour enhanced by the sunshine was breathtakingly beautiful. My heart started to beat faster, my soul fully rejoiced and my face lit up like the radiant sun.

The freedom that Kahlid spoke of was with me throughout the day, even with all of the tourists present. Once most had disappeared, my freedom for adventure took me to wandering into the forbidden caves.

While alone in many of the caves, I chanted and danced freely. As I chanted, I listened to the sweet resonances enter my ear, skin, body, and the innermost core of my soul. The acoustics were beyond anything I had experienced before. I realized I felt free, "Forever Free," as Kahlid said. Free from the inside of me.

This freedom Kahlid was speaking about was not only with nature, but also that of the inner soul. It was without attachments to possessions and the entrapments of commercial enterprise. Traditionally, these Bedouins are not attached to their locations or symbols of the outside world. Today, they roam a little less freely than before and they possess some symbols of modern society, but this does not take away their soulful freedom.

After Kahlid and his friend left me, I sat for a bit longer thinking about freedom. Was I free? Were we free? Was I attached to some of these symbols of commercialism that plague the Western world? I began to realize that real freedom goes much deeper than the surface. It is innate and lives happily in our cells. Freedom is within everyone. It is the basis of our existence. Freedom is the breath that regenerates our souls. Freedom goes deeper inside of us than our external attachments to business, politics, and religious symbols. It is the pure freedom of the soul.

When freedom comes into question, it is often in the form of restrictions, control, and suppression by government, religion, advertising, business, and our own minds. No one can ever take the freedom of our souls away, even though we are seduced and tested into this every second of the day. We have the choice to listen to our inner voice of freedom and use this to empower whatever we want to accomplish in life or to simply "be." We also have the choice to allow our freedom to be dictated by others. Finding the balance between the external and internal is part of the journey.

Using the power of our freedom inside of us gives us immense strength. It can change the world. I look at the spiritual and enlightened leaders like Gandhi and Mandela who challenged their own internal as well as external freedoms to free their people from oppression. Freedom starts within and moves outward.

As youthful as Kahlid was, I found him to be wiser than most people I know. He understood what was important to him in life. It appeared to me that he was not attached to the symbols or attachments of modern society. "Forever Free" begins at home and moves outward into the world.

Before Kahlid joyfully went on his way with his lute under his arm, his last words to me were "I think I will sleep here under the stars tonight. It is going to be a beautiful night. Forever Free."

As I was about to exit ancient Petra with the words of Kahlid resounding in my soul, I noticed the guard at the entry of the Treasury, who had forbidden people to enter, had finally gone off duty. Bedouin children had entered the Treasury and taken up playful residence. They were laughing, playing games, and running around with total abandon. I entered as well and chanted as they danced and played around me with such joy. Their play was such freedom to me and those around!

DISCOVERY

Allow your Self and soul to reflect and resonate the words of Kahlid Aoud Al. Bdoll and Victor Frankl. What is freedom to you? ~ Are you forever free? ~ In your everyday world, how does your freedom manifest? ~ Where does freedom sit within you physically and how does it make you feel? ~ Go to the place in your soul where freedom sits and experience its sweet nectar.

Pearl • **Learning**

Oyster • **New York City, USA**

"The unexamined life is not worth living."

SOCRATES

It was 1979. Hell's Kitchen, midtown Manhattan. I had come to New York City to study contemporary dance at The Ailey School and to teach figure skating at Sky Rink, which was a beautiful ice rink on the sixteenth floor of a venerable building on the corner of 33rd Street and 10th Avenue, an unusual location for a skating rink that, to this day, amuses me. This move to New York City was quite a jump, a leap of faith, for a guy who grew up in a very British, quiet, and quaint neighbourhood of south Oak Bay in Victoria, a city often known as the destination for the "newly wed and nearly dead." Little did I know what was in store for me in the Big Apple.

In my first three months in New York City, I moved four times to various apartments and neighbourhoods. This was an excruciating learning experience in itself because I had to move my suitcases, a futon, and a chair each time in a taxi. I finally settled into an apartment in a dilapidated five-storey walk-up building with my boyfriend.

My introduction to the tenement was to kick in the front door to enter the building, then proceed to walk up to the fourth floor on the smelly, dirty stairs with peeling or torn away linoleum and past the graffiti-covered walls. The door to my apartment had a doorknob hole in it so any passer-by could sneak a peak inside. After opening the door, I heard a rustling sound all around me. What was that? I turned on the lights and I had my first view of the lovely cucarachas scampering away into the walls. I thought, How could anyone be lonely in New York with these creatures?

This was to be my living space for six months, and Hell's Kitchen was certainly an appropriate name for my new neighbourhood. I looked around at the long railroad-style apartment, with room after room connected by a hall. It was dirty and noisy. I went to the toilet and I heard water running above me. I looked up. To my surprise, there was a major hole in the ceiling exposing the pipes from the toilet in the apartment above. I felt tears come to my eyes. What have I come to in my life? What penance am I paying for? Was all this change and learning worth it?

During conversations with my boyfriend, he asked why I had chosen New York. The first answer that came out of my mouth was the opportunity to learn, an "O2L", as I call it.

He was surprised and impressed with my statement and said, "Most people come to the city to use it and abuse it." Primarily, I hungered for dance knowledge, but I also wanted to acquire life experience. And this was the right place to do this at this time in my life, when I was on an insatiable quest for learning.

Every moment of the day I was going into sensory overload with new learning; my eyes were wide open, my sixth sense was stimulated, and I learned to move like crazy. At times I thought I would explode from all the new experiences.

One day I gathered the courage to ask my boyfriend why there was no lock on the front door to the apartment building. He said, "They often put a lock on it, but it's busted within a day or so." The people who would break in were drug addicts. Apparently, I lived on the heroine users' corner and they would go up to the roof and shoot up. I thought, Safe neighbourhood!

These were also the days of my starving artist routine. To earn a living, I taught figure skating at Sky Rink. Now that was an adventure to be on a skating rink that was located on the sixteenth floor! Most of my clients were adult women who liked to ice dance. When I began working there, I was told that I would have to be at the rink twice a week for a dance session called "taxi dancing." I did not understand what this meant at first, but then learned that I was to partner the ladies around the rink for a couple minutes, doing waltzes, foxtrots, and other dances, and being paid per "taxi ride." Hmm, I thought, now what am I?

It was kind of like being a hired guy and sometimes felt like I was prostituting myself. When I was first introduced to this activity I was appalled at what I had reduced myself to. But I was learning! At that time I got, a whopping seventy-five cents a dance. I was exhausted by the end my forty-five minute taxi session because it was as if the ladies clung to me for dear life.

Taxi dancing goes like this. Before the session would begin, women would run to my sign-up board and write their names next to all the dances they wanted with me. My board was always full, thanks to my personality, youthful good looks, and unique dance ability and agility. Every male partner had his own signature of ladies. Sometimes women feuded over those who signed up for more dances than they should with their favourite partner. Observing these skirmishes remains a fond recollection of my time at Sky Rink.

Every day I was learning. It was like the words in the song "New York, New York"—"the city that never sleeps." It never sleeps. Sometimes, I would sit in a restaurant and listen to old actors talking about the good ol' days; listen to waiters who are wanna-be actors trying to "make it or bust"; talk to the occasional street person; attend many different dance classes with the best teachers around; watch incredible dance and theatre performances; and I even could compare the rice puddings from different diners around the city.

I also learned to be economical by ordering hot water and a slice of lemon in restaurants so I didn't have to pay for a tea or by going to Canal Street and find the best bargains in clothes—all so I could afford to take another dance class.

My determination to learn not just contemporary dance technique, but also life, truly led me to experience much, much more. The essential part of learning, I realized, is to open ourselves to it, no matter how old we are—surrender to our O2L, getting under it with passion and support the experience(s) fully. The quest for knowledge, bettering ourselves, and moving toward excellence is why we are here in this body form.

My mother thought my move to New York was ill-advised at best, and in actuality, crazy. The Big Apple proved to be one of my most risky shifts in my life journey, but in reflection, I would do it all over again for that excitement of such hard work, adventure, and knowledge.

NYC was an O2L just as every day of our lives is an O2L. We can choose to see the positive or we can choose to see the negative. To learn, one creates an upward spiral of energy flow, leading toward growth. The opposite leads a downward spiral toward victimization and self-pity. I experienced both of these situations in New York. The city is totally in your face, all the time, and the only way to escape it is to leave the city or go home and lock the many locks on door and breathe a sigh of relief.

When I looked around me, I observed that our challenge in life, if we should accept the challenge, is to keep seeing the bright side of learning, even when all hopes are seemingly lost, or the force of nature is moving against us. Here is where faith comes in. Here is where the rubber hits the road. Dig in and move with the flow. Be conscious of the fact that we are in a learning state all the time, even when we don't think we are. We are always learning, just sometimes not absorbing it totally.

The city never lets up. It is invigorating, exciting, and energizing but exhausting at the same time. I realized a great learning experience one morning. I was tired. My body was physically exhausted from dancing six hours per day, plus teaching. My legs felt as if they were screaming. I stood in my apartment before my door, staring at the hole and the four locks, and thought there must be a better way to learn. I opened the door and as I walked down the stairs, I felt my tired body become tense as I prepared for the madness of the street.

At that moment, I decided this incredible learning period had come to an end. I remembered my father telling me that life is in chapters. Yes, this chapter of learning was over. I must move onto another place of learning. We need to realize and accept this from the heart when it is time to move on.

I moved to Paris a few months later for another O2L.

DISCOVERY

Have you ever thought of situations and decisions in your life as an opportunity to learn, or O2L? ~ What would this do for your motivation and inspiration if you saw them as an O2L? ~ What if you saw even most experiences in life as an O2L? ~ Reflect upon some of the learning moments in your life that stand out for you. How have these added to your performance in life?

Pearl • **Respect**

Oyster • **Bern, Switzerland**

"If one doesn't respect oneself, one can have neither love nor respect for others."

AYN RAND

Gandhi's non-violence policy spoke of the value of respect. Respect toward others without violating their humanity is very important to achieving awareness of our power within. Leading from a position of respect goes a very long way. To respect someone else is the same act as honouring yourself.

I somehow sense that respect has been with me since the beginning of my life. I was particularly struck by the true meaning of respect while working on a large touring skating show in Europe that I choreographed, directed, and wrote.

I arrived at the ice rink in Cardiff, Wales to audition skaters who were already working for the same production company on another show. I put them through a rather grueling test of their talents. They were nervous, frightened, and didn't smile much. It seemed as though they were inviting negativity. Most of them did fairly well, but unfortunately there were others who I did not choose for the forthcoming show.

I did a bit of research to find out how their company had treated them, how long they had been working with the company, and what were their range of talents. At the end of the audition, I had a long conversation with the chosen skaters about the new show and how important they were to making it work.

At that point, I realized from my research and the appearance of their body language and speech that I was inheriting a group of skaters who had lost complete respect for themselves, their talents, and that of the others. The company's managers, performance directors, and previous choreographers and directors treated them without respect for years. I found myself with a cast of unmotivated, sceptical, distrusting, and frightened skaters.

When they arrived in Bern, Switzerland for six weeks of intense rehearsals, I again sensed their uncertainty and nervousness of what they would be asked to do. As a whole, they were defensive and very negative. Some even cowered like children, afraid to speak up.

I sensed from the beginning that if I was going to produce a creative, spectacular, and mindful show, showing motivation and respect for them was the only way for me to foster a cohesive and healthy team. Building this trust would come only from exhibiting consistent behaviour and a steady course of action. For me, this seemed a natural way of being, as this is what I believe in from my inner most soul. I wanted to give them more than a show. I wanted to nurture their integrity, their self-worth, and self-confidence. My brilliant creative team also realized this as we slowly built a supportive group structure.

I started to work toward this goal each morning with a class on ice to perfect their edges, turns, body positions, and much more, not unlike what trained dancers would go through every morning to wake up their bodies. They would glide and weave across the ice in groups of three or more, slowly developing consistency of form and working together in harmony. I used soft music not only to calm them, but also to stimulate their inner beings. As they wove gracefully, breathing with every movement, I would offer supportive comments and corrections, build their confidence of their talents, as well as bring fun and laughter into the day. As the class progressed and became more difficult, so did the tempo of the music and exercises.

At first, they were rather sceptical of this class, but came to realize its importance. Every class ended with a group hug. I would talk to them about the day and I thanked them for their hard work and dedication. To most, this was a massive surprise, as they had never been treated with such respect and positive behaviour. They apparently were waiting for when the yelling and negativity would begin.

As I learned from many of them, they had lost all respect and trust for the company, but needed the job as there weren't many other avenues for them. They felt like they had very few choices in their lives at this point. Many of the international cast came from the former Eastern Bloc countries, which had a reputation for disrespect and negative working situations.

In many ways, I was angry with the company management; I couldn't understand how such disregard for others could be fashioned as a method for control, power, and subsequent profitability. Perhaps I was rather naïve in my thinking, but I knew in my heart what would get these skaters to perform at their potential.

I chatted with each of them, telling them how important they were to making the show happen, and ultimately, it was their show, not mine, to be proud of. Each day, I would give them an intention and speak more and more about the story line of the show. They rapidly began to trust my sincerity. I truly felt that my assistant and myself were simply the catalysts for the creation of the show, and that the skaters were the most important elements who did all the work, in every performance. Therefore, they were the ones where the knowledge and self-respect needed to be embedded.

I also sensed that this respect needed to be spread through the backstage crew as well. They needed to know how important they were. If we all worked together in harmony with a singular defining goal, what power could that bring? From time to time, I would bring them to my meetings with the skaters, as each one of them needed to realize that they were important to the success of the show.

Each day we progressed with the choreography. The classes got better and better. Production number after production number moved forward with learning and precision. Talks continued about the meaning of the story and roles that people were to play. Focus was vital and a steady time line to opening night was kept on course.

What I began to observe over the six to eight weeks of rehearsal was a wonderful sense of warmth, respect, happiness, and self-confidence. It was growing daily and they were becoming more like a family. They began to trust each other and find their truth again. They rebuilt confidence in their skating and it improved immensely from the challenges that I gave them. They smiled and laughed more and more. I also encouraged them to speak up and ask questions of themselves and others.

When veterans from other shows and staff from head office would come to view rehearsals, they were very impressed. In fact, some would say that there was something wrong. I would ask, "What do you mean, wrong?" They would say things like, "Where is the yelling, screaming, and tension on the ice or back stage?" They thought the show was definitely not right without this type of behaviour. I would smile at such a ridiculous comment and say, "We are ahead of schedule. Everyone is happy, and we are working hard."

As the work environment blossomed, word got out to the other skaters within the company. This show became the envy of the other touring shows. Of course, not all the cattiness and back-biting was eliminated, but they learned to deal with it with grace and would speak up if there was a problem.

I sensed from some of the management that they didn't like the cast's new-found confidence. They seemed to be still stuck in their old ways of managing people. They had not grown or changed with the new sense of collective ownership that the performers had found. They still relied on their old ways of persuasion, but now that had not been working so well. Luckily, the executive producer, who was, bar none, phenomenal, supported and protected me from the management.

Regardless of whether the touring management changed or the company itself, the performers had changed, and now held onto a renewed respect for themselves and others. Years later, I found out that this show was a major turning point in many of their lives.

Opening night came and the performance was brilliant. The energy was so powerful in this show; it was magical. The standing ovations were loud and supportive. The skaters were full of joy and pride. They were proud of their show like no others before. They had pushed themselves technically, creatively, emotionally, and grown spiritually for weeks and the pay off was now here. They skated from the heart and knew no one could take this moment from them. These once unmotivated and fearful people I began working with months before were now transformed to confident and strong beings. They produced a powerful show and they realized only they could do this.

The last day I was with them was a sad but very happy moment for me. I told them that the show was officially now theirs, so it was their responsibility to take care of it, respect it, and respect themselves and others.

Months later, some of the company management spoke to me about the unique cohesiveness that was created and what a pleasure it was for them to watch this show. The production also had created fewer problems among the skaters because they were happy with their work. The company felt they could rely on the consistency of this show's performance—on and off the ice. This show became the envy of the company's other touring shows.

I come back to Gandhi who respected all whether they followed him or not. Because of his unflinching respect for human freedom, among other values, India won its independence. We can all do our own part in our own way to preserve respect and perhaps stimulate the independence it can bring people.

Now when I meet with the people I worked with in this show, we greet each other with joy and love. We realize the bond we created together and how special this time was. It will go on for a very long. It was an experience that was created with passion. We realize that the trust and respect for each other remains just as strong as it was many years before.

Respect yourself as you would respect others.

DISCOVERY

Is respect a value that is important to you? ~ How does respect play out in your life? ~ Think of a situation where respect was not visible or apparent you, and think of a time when it was. How did you respond? ~ Where did you feel your response to this in your body? ~ What is the response you want for yourself and for others?

Pearl • **Legacy**

Oyster • **Calgary, Canada**

"Begin with the end in mind."

STEPHEN COVEY

The 1988 Calgary Winter Olympic Games was my first *Aha* realization of what "legacy" can mean. I had been honoured to be chosen to choreograph and direct the closing ceremonies. It was a once-in-a-lifetime experience and I embraced it, every nerve racking and ecstatic moment. The production and creative team who I worked with were exemplary. We equally gave from our hearts and souls and received back, if not more, from this experience.

Have you ever walked on a beach and left footprints in the sand? When you are looking back at those footprints behind, you see that they are also coming toward you. That is what legacies are like—leaving footprints in the sand. No matter what we perform, do, or say, we are leaving footprints. Those footprints may physically be lost when the water passes over them, like cleaning the slate, but they remain in your heart and the hearts of others, forevermore.

I invite you to experience those footprints with me as I recreate this special moment in time and realize the power of legacy.

Imagine a chilly winter's evening as you sit in the open-aired McMahon Stadium, Calgary, Canada, filled with 60,000 people, including most of the Olympic athletes. The sound of partying is in the air: the human wave circulates the stadium; 60,000 candles flicker like stars in the night; the Olympic flame blazes and dances above the stadium; and in the middle of the stadium is an ice surface the size of two Olympic ice rinks. The stadium feels as if it is going to levitate and take off into space. The energy is electrifying. The performers, the many amateur skaters from ages three to seventy, sit nervously in tents and dressing rooms, waiting their time to skate into the stadium. The ceremonies begin with grand aplomb.

An hour before the start time, with butterflies in my stomach, I made my way to the backstage tents and dressing rooms to thank the performers all for their dedicated work. I encouraged them to complete this once-in-a-lifetime experience, one which they would never repeat again.

The nervousness in the air was palpable, ferociously mixed with incredible adrenalin and patriotism. They knew the force of the nation was with them, as well as their own personal achievement. It was now or never, no turning back on their personal legacy they would leave for themselves, and be part of a bigger legacy for generations of sportsmen, Canadians, and people worldwide. This legacy would ultimately come in the form of sport venues, community spirit, national honour, personal successes and emotions, and much more.

When we had begun the rehearsal period six months earlier, I told them, "I do not know what you can expect to feel, but it will be something you have not experienced in your life before and perhaps will not again, but the power of this will last with you. Your legacy to Calgary, Canada, the athletes, and the Olympics will be felt not only by yourself, but others for a long time to come."

The fanfare music began, the announcer welcomed everyone, and the show commenced with one skater skating into the stadium with the Olympic flag, preceding the flags of others countries following. Once those skaters hit the ice, I had never ever seen them perform to such precision and brilliance. The crowd went mad, and the stamping of feet on the bleachers resounded through the night air.

They were apprehensive, as most had never performed in their lives and, definitely, never on such a large ice surface in front of so many people. Can you imagine the rush of adrenaline when they entered the stadium to the incredible sound of the audience? I had no idea how it really was for them, it is one of those moments beyond words. But I felt, sitting high above in the sound booth, a total heat rise inside my body of euphoria intermixed with some nerves, of course. It was an incredible sensation throughout my body and my heart.

The ceremony continued for almost two hours and with many

different production numbers and the obligatory protocol elements woven seamlessly together with the creative performance. When the show was over and the audience left, many skaters hung around on the ice not wanting to leave. I rapidly made my way down to the ice to celebrate and thank them for such an amazing accomplishment.

Their bodies were dancing with smiles, radiating from the deepest place in their hearts. As we hugged and gathered together, the most common statement to me was, "You were right, you could never have prepared us for this moment of ecstasy." That was part of the legacy I wanted to leave for them. It was the incredible moment of success, self-achievement, and contribution to a nation's honour.

Every one of those skaters who went on the ice that night, returned to the dressing rooms a changed person on so many levels. You could see that their hearts opened up, perhaps more than ever before. Their starry eyes were big, shiny, and happy, and a resounding rhythm danced throughout their bodies.

They performed better than they ever thought they could. Many said to me that when they stepped onto the ice in the stadium and saw the candles flickering and the ecstatic noise of the audience, they thought they would faint from the excitement. They knew deep inside what this incredible moment in time meant for them, Calgary, Canada, and the world. Throughout their whole bodies, minds, and souls they had given and received so much.

The closing ceremonies was a momentous event in my life and for all the performers, assistants, and technical and creative departments. Our mandate was to give the world a show they would remember forever. That was our combined legacy.

Legacy doesn't necessarily have to be left behind by only famous people such as Martin Luther King or Gandhi, or a CEO or politician. You can leave multiple legacies all along the way of your life, or be part of other people's legacies. You can create legacies as a parent who has a child or as a writer, as well as someone who is part of great philanthropic events.

Have you ever considered this thought? We are all creating legacies. We are leaving something behind that will touch others in many different ways, tangibly and intangibly. Having a legacy in mind or being conscious of what you want to leave behind is a great place to begin. This can give you a greater purpose and direction for what you want to do or reach.

When you have set a legacy of intention for a project, your children, your work, and/or your life, you can use it to energize, motivate, and spur you to great heights. Having a legacy in mind and working from the heart sets a well-informed direction toward achievement. Yes, sometimes life gets in the way, but that should not be the determining factor to what you want to achieve.

Why wait to leave a legacy till when you are dead; why not experience it along the road of life? What are your many legacies? How would it feel if you made it a living, conscious entity while you are still so vibrantly alive? *Aha*!

When I came on board the Olympic ceremonies team, I was made aware of the legacy that the Calgary Olympics wanted to leave for the athletes, sport, the city, and its people, wherever they came from. The official organizing committee had their own overlying bequest for the Games, as does the official charter of the Olympic Games. There is inheritance on all levels. I needed to determine my legacy for the Games as well. My legacy was to give my performers, my team, Canada, the world, and athletes a once-in-a-lifetime experience. I wanted to receive the fulfillment of having accomplished such a large feat. I wanted to be proud to be Canadian and proud of my performers and team. In fact, it was the first time in my life I actually felt pride of being Canadian. This changed my life.

The results of a common legacy brought cohesion, mission, and purpose to everyone's work, which was for the common good of all, no matter how many conflicts and disagreements happened along the way. Even to this day, many years later, whenever I meet someone from this event, we are instantly reconnected from the heart and transported back to those amazing last moments of the ceremony, when kd lang rocked the socks off the whole stadium to "Turn Me Round."

When the dust finally settled and all the athletes and tourists had left the city, we began to realize the legacy that was left throughout Calgary as a result of the Olympic Games. Even today when people recall the Olympics, it is proudly remembered with incredible smiles on their faces, as the memories have woven into their lives. The footprints are alive and well.

DISCOVERY

What does legacy mean to you? ~ It may not seem important to you at this point in your life, but I encourage you to reflect upon this. What would it do for your situations in life, whether it involves family, friends, work, or more? ~ How would it motivate or inspire these situations? ~ What is the legacy you would like to create today?

15TH PEARL

Pearl • **Intuition**

Oyster • **St. Petersburg, USA**

*"You
must train your
intuition – you must trust
the small voice inside you
which tells you exactly what to
say, what to decide."*

INGRID BERGMAN

I was heading off to choreograph and direct what I perceived to be my next figure skating extravaganza that would propel me to international figure skating stardom. On departing from Victoria, British Columbia, Canada to St Petersburg, Florida, USA where rehearsals were about to start, I said to my mother, "Mum, I can't wait for this to be over."

For me, this is the story about how hitting rock bottom can transform your life. It led me to so many changes and realizations. This is the story of finding my heart. It is the story about what happens when I do not listen to my intuition. Most lives have turning points; this was the single most profound turning point in my life.

I was asked to adapt a famous stage and screen production for a figure skating performance. The producer told me that he wanted to create a new contemporary look for this show and possibly change the creative direction of his company. This challenge was extremely exciting for me, and put my heart and soul into developing the adaptation.

Although we had some initial discussion regarding our differences in stylistic preference and personal taste, he agreed to develop my concept. For the next five months, I energetically worked with the creative team: a costume/set designer from the Toronto area; the original music composer from Los Angeles; auditions with skaters from around the US and Canada; and creative presentation meetings at the company's headquarters in Washington, D.C. The creative process was stimulating and very exciting. I felt like this was going to be a magnificent, ground-breaking show.

At different times during these early months of creation, the producer reminded me, "You know, we don't have the rights to the story yet, but we will get them." One sunny day in early May, I got a phone call from the producer telling me that the rights had been denied. My heart dropped, my world felt as if it had just been pulled out from underneath me. What exactly did this all mean? What was I going to do now? All of a sudden my life was abruptly put on hold.

Although I initially was interested in this particular production only, I was invited to consider producing an alternative creative property. The producer insisted that I was the "man for the job," but I was confused. My intuition was speaking. I reminded him we were working against time and a decision needed to be made regarding what properties he wanted to develop. But he could not give me a firm answer. I said that I really needed to have some time to think about this change in direction. He was generous and said, "Take your time."

I carefully considered my decision. Was I to say yes before the new properties were decided upon, or was I to wait? Waiting would not be fair at all to the company at this late date. I searched my mind for the reasons I would continue to stay with the project. I decided that I could still put my best creative power to work, but it basically came down to money. Money first, creativity second, heart third. So what did I do? I bit the bullet and went for the contract, thinking, "Yes, I can still create a great show."

After my approval, we went into overdrive and hyper-speed pre-production. I spent time in Los Angeles, considering various potential properties. All the stories and characters appeared to be the same. By the end of two agonizing days of research and consideration, I made a decision. I gingerly asked if I could adapt the creativity and music of the properties to more contemporary beats, musically and choreographically. I knew well that the company had a very strict policy on their characters and how they were to be represented. Luckily, they allowed some room for interpretation.

The travel now accelerated. I could sense fatigue building, plus something else which I ignored constantly—the voice from within, the voice of my intuition. All this travel increased my tension and nervousness. My lower back began to exert its powerful voice. A bad attack of sciatica took up residence within me and I could barely sit down. It was painful to sit on a plane, on a chair, anywhere. When I was in meetings in San Diego with the music arranger, my only relief was to lie down on the floor, remain standing, or constantly move around. Was my intuition telling me something that I was not listening to?

As time rapidly passed, I could sense the producer and his in-house director getting very nervous about the direction of the show. I was beginning to get a bit thrown off creatively and began to doubt myself.

Pre-rehearsals began in Victoria with a small group of enthusiastic performers, my line captains, my assistant choreographer, and the fearless project manager. I was beginning to sense a "dis-ease" within me about my work. Was I being insecure about my decisions and choreography, or was I fed up with the craziness that was building around me from the top brass, or was this the typical creative stress that goes along with productions? I suspect it was a bit of everything, but I also sensed something deeper at play.

Our early rehearsal period in Victoria ended and the company proceeded to St Petersburg for final rehearsals. This stage went very well, the skaters worked hard, and as always, I made sure that I encouraged excellence and happiness.

The atmosphere was glowing and the skaters were getting more and more excited about the new challenges. All was heading in the right direction and I was oblivious to anything that might be happening in the background. I was on time with my schedule and was focused beyond belief. However, I began to sense some noise from the upper management that I wasn't moving fast enough.

I was told on the third Saturday into rehearsals that the producer and his in-house director were coming the following Monday morning. He wanted to see a run-through of the show.

I was nervous, of course, and so were the skaters. Something inside of me was not sitting well and I couldn't put my finger on it at all. I recall sensing a distance from the producer and his director. What was that distance? The skaters were doing their best and the choreography was rather messy, but that is usual at this point in rehearsals. When the run-through was over, I could feel the tension from all the powers around me. I was then called into an office. The producer was generous at first and asked me what I was going to do with certain elements of the show. Then the bomb dropped. He said, "I don't like the show." I was then sitting on the opposite side of the desk, trembling, tired, and without much fight. He said he would give me one-and-a-half days to do a series of changes. I told him what changes were possible and what were not.

I left the office shaking, stunned, confused, and wondering if I should panic. I went to my change room and cried, thinking, Where do I go from here? What will I do? I had a responsibility to the skaters and to the company. I was committed and had signed a contract. I gathered myself together and created a plan with my project manager and assistants. We dug ourselves in, rallied the forces, and divided up the work for the next day and a half.

The producer arrived at the appointed time to see the changes. I had prepared the skaters and told them of the possible consequences. I could sense their nervousness. It seemed the moment of reckoning had come. The changes were to be judged. The skaters did their best. The response was quiet. The producer and in-house director left for a meeting. I waited for what seemed to be hours and perhaps a lifetime. I was then called in to the office. The producer was forceful and right to the point. He said something like, "I don't like the show and it doesn't work for me." He wanted me to pack my bags, demanding that I leave immediately through the back door without speaking to anyone. He said he would have a meeting with the cast and crew to tell them I was no longer with the show.

I left his office seriously wounded, speechless, and in tears. I was so angry. My project manager, performance director, and assistant choreographer came into the room. They were waiting to hear the verdict on the show. I told them the news and they were totally dumbfounded at this turn of events. We were all confused and crying. I looked at their wet eyes and thanked them for all their hard work and told them it was up to them now. They could do it.

I packed, left through the back door, and got into my rented car and drove to the ocean. I took a long walk along the beach, with the Gulf of Mexico soothing my feet. I was in no shape to talk to anyone about anything. I felt I had just completely lost my world. I blamed myself completely, then I blamed the producer. I hated him for doing this to me. The rush of all negative thoughts and voices raced through my mind, body, and soul, and my protective mechanism took over in full force. I took this situation totally personally and was devastated. I believed I was a failure.

Within a day, I heard that the producer had dismissed my assistant choreographer and costume/set designer. They all were to leave as soon as possible. A dark cloud seemed to hang over the production.

Before I left the city, I did finally end up going to the ice rink to say my goodbyes to the skaters, crew, and assistants. I told them they needed to respect the producer's decision and not to take sides, as that does not help the situation. I told them how proud I was of them and to move forward and create the most wonderful show they could. I felt a lot of love from the cast, crew, and my faithful assistants. That was more important to me than the job itself. Tears began to flow.

I guess I got my wish of "I can't wait until this is over." Although, this was not the way I wanted it to end or even dreamed it of ending. When this happened, so many thoughts rushed through my physical being. I truly thought I would never work again. I had lost my courage, my sense of self-respect, my spirit. I was drained physically, mentally, emotionally, and spiritually. I had lost my way.

For the next six months, I slowly went through a discovery and reflection process. Every step I took felt so fragile, but getting stronger each day. I read books, talked to people, took courses in film and religiously followed the book *The Artist's Way* by Julia Cameron.

Pure happiness came out of those months of recovery. My spirit was healthy and alive again, full of inspired energy to create. I reflected back on my experience and knew I had done my best at the time to create a great show. I became thankful that the producer had fired me. It may sound strange, but it is true. He had taught me a very valuable lesson about intuition.

I finally came to the realization why my body was ailing so badly and also why I had said that I couldn't wait until it was over. Why? It was a result of not listening to the voice of my intuition. I was deaf to those words and I had drowned any reason for my body's pain. I was not living from my heart. I was putting other aspects first, such as money and ego. When I realized this, I rejoiced wholeheartedly. I then vowed I would never agree to do another job, or anything in fact, without listening to my intuition.

Ten years later I found myself living in Belgium. Ironically, the ill-fated production came to Brussels and some of the skaters were the same people I had worked with in the show. I invited them to dinner. They told me how much working with me those few short weeks had changed their lives and taught them so much. They told me how over the years I had become an icon for the inspiration of the show and this still continues. I had no idea this had happened. I humbly smiled and my heart jumped a beat.

I may have sensed I was not listening to my intuition enough during that whole escapade, but it seemed others were touched and learned through this experience. In fact, we all learned so much, but in different ways.

Since that day, I have not taken another job or contract without tuning into my intuition. My intuition has led me and I have listened to it, as well as to my mind, body, and soul.

Listen to your intuition.
Allow the boom-boom of your heart to
Resound with joy and love.
Wake up to the sweet scent of fragrance of your heart.
It is there for you to live, learn, and dance, as
Your intuition is deep in your spirit speaking to you.
Be one with your intuition, NOW.

DISCOVERY

Take a few moments to think about intuition. Do you listen to your intuition? ~ How important for you is it to listen to your intuition? ~ What has listening to your heart taught you? ~ How does this make you feel? ~ Reach down deep and listen to your intuition— the voice of the soul.

Pearl • **Listening**

Oyster • **Sitges, Spain**

*"The
first duty of love is
to listen."*

PAUL TILLICH

The traumatic work experience that had happened in St Petersburg, Florida triggered a journey of self-discovery to find the greater purpose of my life. Having been fired from a large skating show contract made me feel as though my world had come to an end. Of course it had not. In fact, it was just the beginning of a new world in which I would discover the pearl of listening.

This period of life had become a time of honest reflection, a turning point in my life. It was an opportunity to find a new and deeper truth for my existence, of discovering who I really am and what I really wanted, which was a much bigger picture than what I had imagined for so many years before. I sensed there was much more to learn and I was thirsty for awareness and knowledge. There is a saying that when the student is ready, the teacher will follow.

One winter day, I was standing on the corner of Burrard and Davie Streets in Vancouver, when a thought crossed my mind, I should contact a friend of mine and ask him about the Indian meditation tradition that he follows. Low and behold, I turned my head to my left and there stood the friend I was thinking of. One may call this serendipity or coincidence. But I see it as the student was ready, the teacher was appearing.

I asked my friend if he had time to chat and answer some questions about the meditation tradition he followed. He said, "What about right now?"

For some time, I had wanted to know more about meditation; it was something I had been interested in, but thought it was not for me. It was now something I wanted to discover, and I now had the opportunity to explore it.

After our conversation, he invited me to a celebration the next night. At the celebration, I discovered there was going to be a meditation retreat in Spain with the Guru of the lineage my friend belonged to during the same time I was to be in Europe. I went home and researched the retreat further and found out it happened to be in Sitges, Spain, a place I had wanted to visit for some time.

I became more curious. For some reason, I sensed I was being drawn to this journey from a voice inside of me. It seemed as though many pieces of the puzzle of my journey were falling into place. I decided to actively listen to what my intuition was saying to me.

The retreat dates coincided perfectly with the beginning of my European trip. However, when booking my return travel date back to Canada, I had some trouble finding availability. I wanted to leave London for Canada on May 3rd, no luck—4th, no luck—5th, no luck—6th,yes, confirmed. I wondered why making this usually easy booking was difficult.

After arriving in Barcelona, I boarded the train and travelled south to Sitges. The train wound its way along the rocky Mediterranean coast, passing in and out of the many tunnels. The sea was dancing with diamonds as the early spring sun beat down upon it. The beauty and the serenity were mesmerizing.

Then, all of a sudden, as I gazed at the sea I heard poetry being recited. I looked around. I could see no one reciting poetry. Strange, I thought, it was coming from me, inside my mind. In fact, it radiated throughout my body. I shook my head to wake myself out of this state, but it persisted. This was a totally unusual situation for me; it had never happened before. And I had never recited, written, or really read poetry in my life.

On arriving in Sitges, the poetry did not stop. I decided to surrender and listen to it.

After checking in at the hotel, I went for a stroll on the boardwalk along the Mediterranean Sea. I saw a beautiful old church and sat on its front stairs. From there, I watched the sea and the sun, felt the gentle breeze caress my skin, and I began to write. Poetry seemed to flow gracefully out of my mind, through my pen, and onto the paper, resonating nature and my inner soul.

Later, I registered at the retreat and attended many sessions on meditation, chanting, and yogic philosophy. I even had the honour of being presented to the Guru. What a magical experience that was. There seemed be a stream of intoxicating calm and loving energy that flowed from her very being. I wanted to somehow have this state.

For me, the overriding theme of her talks was the resounding principle of listening. It stuck inside of me so profoundly. In fact, it became my new mantra—listen. It just kept repeating inside of me, even when I least expected it.

The Guru spoke about listening as an active, not passive, voice. Listening is not just sitting around and waiting for something to happen, no, it takes conscious effort. She spoke about asking questions and sending them forth to the universe, and then trusting and staying alert for the answers.

Near the end of my stay, I was asked if I wanted to take a two-day intensive course with the Guru at the end of the retreat. I declined. After five days, I was already full with information and a deeper sense of being and listening. I now needed time to reflect on what I had experienced.

Then someone said to me, "Why don't you go to the intensive in London, May 3rd–5th?" I was immediately in shock when I heard this—I couldn't get a flight from London back to Canada on those dates. What I had just heard went way beyond my comprehension. A voice inside me said, "Is this the reason that I couldn't get a flight back to Canada on those days?" What was going on? This was odd to me. So, I took this as a sign to listen, and I signed up for the intensive in London.

Something very unusual seemed to be happening, but I decided not fight it. I sensed something was definitely moving inside of me that was perhaps bigger than me. The important thing was, I was listening with intent to the signals and flowing with it all. Yes, freely flowing, as a river, gathering information on the way to the ocean. I was now very curious as to where my journey was leading. So I listened more and followed my instincts and voices inside.

By being open and listening to the voice within back in Vancouver, I had found a profound, wise, living master. I was now ready and ripe to listen intelligently and savour the wisdom of my supportive spiritual teacher, who, I have since found, is my guide to the discovery of my deeper knowledge, greater awareness of my spirit, and overall universal understanding. My teacher, my Guru, my coach (in many ways) has assisted me to open up to a bigger picture, bigger universe, inside and out. I was now truly ready to listen as I continued my journey to my heart, my soul. Yes, I had found my teacher and I am sure that in life I will find more teachers. How exciting that will be. Ask and you will receive, but pay attention to what you ask for, because you just may get it!

My days in Sitges and the intensive in London were profound and curious at the same time. I sometimes felt like an outsider looking in on many people who had already started their studies of life. I was always invited in with love and support, with the knowledge that the teacher opens the door, gives you knowledge, and shares wisdom, then it is your practice, your responsibility, to find your own answers and experiences.

The poetry continued to flow as I took the train back to Barcelona to continue my travels in Europe. I later learned, that the manifestation of my poetry came from a bigger picture of my energetic awakening. It was part of me wanting from my heart to discover and listen to the greater universe within me, which also radiated to the world outside of me.

Listening is just so sweet.
It is tender.
It is fierce with courage.
It is so quiet and silent most of the time.
Open to the flow inside and outside.

Be one with listening,
As the voices are real.
They come from a deeper space
Bigger than us,
But it is us.
There is no time like NOW
To listen to the sweetness
And
Fragrance
Of
The power of
Listening.
Listen and ye shall find the truth.

My practice of listening has continued and changed the direction of my life. It has directly impacted the choices I make with a greater awareness and consciousness. I am so happy for this practice I have been awakened to.

Listen to your internal environment.
Listen to your external environment.
Listen to the deepest voices.
Listen to your senses.
Listen to your heart.
There lies the wisdom of knowledge.

DISCOVERY

Have you ever concentrated on listening intently from the heart? ~ Are you ready to listen? ~ What do you think this would do for you if you did? ~ Find a time in your life when you really experienced the art of deep, inner listening. What did you hear, see, and feel? ~ How has this changed your life or even that momentary situation? ~ Start listening friend, it will change your life.

Pearl • **Mirror**

Oyster • **Lisbon to Porto, Portugal**

"Life is
like a mirror, we
get the best results when
we smile at it."

ANONYMOUS

As we look outward, we see
The radiant sun, warm, sparkling
Full of peace spreading
His male strength, courage, love, and peace.
He exists inside of us all
Both male and female, young and old.

What we are seeing outside is the
Mirror of the heart, the soul, the inner Spirit,
The sun within.

One sunny, crisp early winter morning, I was waiting at the Oriente train station for the high-speed express train to take me from Lisbon to Porto in the north of Portugal. The sun was shining beautifully, creating figurative shadows on the platform set in the unique architecture of the train station, which resembles glass sails of a ship.

It was a couple of days after New Year's Day, 2006. I was going to meet friends of mine who had recently moved to Porto. Shortly after the train left the station and I was gazing out of the window, a voice inside of my head said, "You are a reflection of everything you are seeing." I looked around and wondered where this voice had actually come from.

I quietly sat and stared out of the window for the whole trip, it was as if the nature, homes, buildings, trees, farmland, construction sites, cars, people, and everything were speaking to me. Yes, the mirror I was looking at was outside my window and the reflection was a metaphoric image of my total self. I thought, How is this so?

The sun beat down on the Tagus River and I realized that the water, with all its power and majesty, was the blood that runs through my veins.

I would see the beautiful, bare trees in the rolling countryside, and saw they were my veins and arteries. The soil, the earth, was my flesh.

Many differently coloured, shaped, and sized houses and buildings speckled the countryside, the villages, and cities. They reminded me of the boxes in my mind. Yes, the many boxes that keep me organized but also, at times, the boxes that contain me in a confused and constricted state of being.

When I saw an open barn door or an open window of a house, I saw this was the way out of my boxes to the expanded state of consciousness. I saw a women lean out of a window to hang her laundry then she closed the window. I felt this was the fear inside of me, that I didn't have the courage to step out of my paradigms. The fear was too strong. My mind was sending a message: Please open the window so I can get out and be free.

The sun shone so brightly in the sky and made me so hot as I sat inside the train. I began to feel as though my insides were burning. I felt as though the light was penetrating into my heart; or was it that the light within me was meeting the light from the outside? The two suns married and triggered the vital energy within my body to dance. The two became one.

The train stopped at a village. On the platform, I saw a very ugly man with a deformed body and face. I thought, "Oh how ugly, how sad for this person, what a shame someone has to be so ugly." Then I thought, "What is my mind saying?" Perhaps there was something ugly inside of me that I didn't want to accept or confront. Maybe it was a repressed emotion or something that someone had said to me. This window was definitely a mirror image of me. Now the question would be to discover who that was being reflected.

Our heart within, is what we see when we look outside,
The heart outside.

We may see love, we may see violence,
We may see anger, we may see happiness,
We may see sadness and so forth.
These emotions outside are a reflection or consequence of
what we sense, feel, or hear
inside of us.

I saw the shadow of my foot on the floor of the train and I stared at it. The shadow moved so gracefully when I moved my foot and became still when I was still. I thought, What is this shadow? What is in a reflection? It is black versus white, dark versus light. Perhaps it is the shadow side of our mind, body, and soul.

The universe outside is reflecting back at us inside,
the Self, the space, the openness, the raw truth, life.

Oh, the ying and yang of the environment that I was seeing, as I looked at the different vegetation change during the three-hour trip, seeing the rolling countryside change to flat lands, with some hills in the distance; to villages of blue, yellow, celadon green; pink homes and buildings; cities of various sizes and period architecture; and people of all ages walking, sitting, running, and wearing all different types of clothing.

I thought, there are so many people of different ages who live in one environment, as do so many different emotions and responses to conversations. How do they all exist in such harmony? Amazing really! They all represent to us a mirror of our whole life and the wisdom that sustains us.

We have the choice to ignore this mirror
Or,
We have the choice to look at the mirror and go
Hmm, what does this reflect or represent within me?

The world outside of us is a mirror of the change that happens over our lifetime. It varies, it changes, constant human change is that mirror, and yet, it seems some things just never change; they simply reflect the same old thing over and over again. When will we wake up to see that our mirror is facing us every second of our lives? The mirror is what keeps us on the ball, alert. Listen and observe all the things with love.

I arrived in Porto with a new way of looking at life and everything that was in front and inside of me. I met my friends and in this mirror, I saw love.

Although, through my life, I have thought about this idea of the mirror and the reflection, it never struck home so profoundly as it did at this Aha moment. I finally listened. I realized it was time to treat everything in life with greater respect and loving thanks for the lessons. However, our everyday life often gets in the way and we don't think like this all the time. But, hopefully, an awareness of the mirror will flash in front of you from time to time. The mirror is in front of us 24/7 and we can be numb or awake to it. I feel it is best to be aware. Don't you?

Be kind to yourself and others.
In all situations
send love out
as the messenger first

and then respond with love
as your support system.

DISCOVERY

Have you ever thought about what you might be mirroring? ~ What are the metaphors your mirror is showing to you? ~ It may not seem very obvious at all, but then, when you think about it, it might? ~ Search for a deeper answer inside, reflect on the mirror so that you can address some changes you may want to make in your life.

18TH PEARL

Pearl • **Smile**

Oyster • **Bali, Indonesia**

"We
shall never know
all the good that a simple
smile can do."

MOTHER TERESA

I arrived in Bali two months after September 11th, 2001. The island felt deserted; there were very few tourists during this troubled time. This was certainly a very good reason for the Balinese not to smile, as their economy is primarily dependent on the tourist trade. Without the tourist trade, the people would suffer greatly. However, for the Balinese, that is not their nature. They are the epitome of sweet gentle smiles, full of spirit, light, and sunshine.

I was asked by many Balinese, "Why aren't the tourists coming to our beautiful paradise?" I told them because in the West we are told to avoid travelling to any Muslim country. They said, "We are Hindu and peace loving." I said, "This doesn't matter. You are part of Indonesia, which is a majority Muslim country." They were challenged by this thought.

Even with this huge dilemma facing them, one of the first things that attracted me to the Balinese was being greeted with smiles wherever I went. It seemed as if their smiles were coming directly from their hearts. Wherever I went, to the shops, hotels, restaurants, temples, or sightseeing; or seeing my personal driver and the children running alongside of the car waving and smiling; or attending dance and music performances and festivals or funerals—people all smiled. Not just little smiles, but full-bodied smiles that exuded from all their pores.

At first, I was sceptical about this, as I thought there must be an agenda. Regardless, it simply felt great to smile. In that, there was a delightful naïveté that transcended into the heart.

I thought, What is the cost of a smile? What does a smile give to you? How do you feel when you smile?

A smile is what the heart does when it pumps life into you.
Be its outward reflection.

It doesn't cost anything to smile. Just look around you, wherever you are, and reflect upon how many people are actually smiling from their hearts. Sadly, few people truly smile from within.

With all the problems mounting in the world, the Balinese simply smiled. The smiles started early in the morning when you begin to greet people. You see women and men making offerings of lovely flowers, incense, and prayers to the gods for prosperity and well-being in front of stores, hotels, houses, and temples. The fragrance of beautifully scented flowers wafted through the air. How could you not smile when you experience this genuine beauty?

In Bali, I met the many classes of society and they all smiled. They connected to a deeper meaning in life and a spirit within them. Their deep-rooted beliefs and value systems are founded in their devotion to their Hindu culture, which honours the self, the heart, and their many gods.

Their culture and faith also asks of them to donate part of their income to the temples, plus contribute to the festivals, parades, and celebrations. Wherever you travel on the island, there are celebrations everyday. This can be extremely stressful for them and especially when tourism is slow. They may complain about their situation like anyone else, but they seem to smile freely through it all. The keyword here is "free." It costs nothing to smile and to laugh. These are the two richest gestures that we can give ourselves in life.

A smile is what the heart does when it pumps life into you.
Be its outward reflection.

I was extremely happy to be in Bali with the calmness it presented to me while other parts of the world were in a state of crazy-making, pre-war build-up. The smiles contributed greatly to this feeling of contentment. Smiles and laughter warm you tenderly. They just make you feel so good inside. They are like the comfort of a mother's womb, friendly, loving, and heartfelt.

Smiling starts from the heart and perhaps that is where we are going wrong in the West. I began to wonder why we seem to be so focused on the mind and so disconnected from our hearts as well as our bodies. Connecting to the heart and leading from the heart gives us personal power, more motivation, energy, and much more.

We take ourselves too seriously. For example, we are often so wrapped up in our self-importance; we indulge in victimization, our poverty, or wealth, or even our reliance on others to make our lives free. It doesn't matter what the situation is in life, from the beggar on the street to the factory worker, CEO, or the richest person in the land, smiling from the heart costs nothing and can be shared by all.

Maybe the Balinese and other smiling cultures can teach us something about life, real life, and the bigger picture. They believe in reincarnation so, for them, this lifetime is only one of many. Maybe this is one of their keys to smiling, laughter, and happiness—this life is just one of many.

I remember telling a new friend in this magical Pacific paradise island how sad I was to leave such a place full of smiling spirits. He wondered why. I told him I was returning back to Canada and other Western nations, where smiling can have many agendas. I explained that, often when you smile at people on the street, they will look away, give you an angry look, lower their heads, or possibly send back verbal obscenities or even attack you. Very rarely will people return the smile with one from their heart.

He looked perplexed, shocked, and naïvely asked why would anyone do this. For him and most Balinese, smiling was as natural as the trees and flowers that grace their existence. It is a reflection of their inner spirit.

It is never too late to smile.
Why not begin now?
There is no better time, as there is no tomorrow until it is here.
Do you want to suddenly get caught dying without a smile?
That I doubt.

The Balinese, like many other cultures and countries I have visited, such as India, Thailand, Mexico, and Central America, all smile freely, as an ongoing daily occurrence. They don't have to think about it because it just happens. Can we take a lesson? I have found smiling usually occurs among people who do not "have" much in the way of finances or possessions. So, what does this say? Even all the money in the world doesn't bring smiles or complete happiness.

Give a smile today to someone you love, someone you don't know, someone you work with, and someone you don't particularly like. Start your own smile revolution and see how you feel about life. Ah—doesn't that feel great?

Open your heart and
Let the smile come forth.
Be open and giving,
Willing to share
Of the spirit, your heart.
That is the real you.
Just get out of the way,
Yes, out of the way now
And let the sunshine through,
Smile!

Ahhh, there it is, the sunshine,
Your heart,
You,
Your spirit.
Now don't you feel better?
Smile and pass it on to everyone
NOW, not later
As there is no later.
Smile now
And you will sense the results immediately.
Just get out of the way, NOW,
And
SMILE.

I left Bali smiling and probably with a few more lines on my face to show for it. What a breath of fresh air that has entered my heart via these Balinese people. Smile!

DISCOVERY

Let yourself smile and just sense what if feels like in your body, mind, and soul. What does it do to your energetic state? ~ What does or can it do for your performance in life? ~ Take a look around you and send a smile to someone. What is the response? ~ Take nothing personally, just smile.

19TH PEARL

Pearl • **Passion**

Oyster • **Monte Carlo, Monaco**

*"Nothing
great in the
world has ever been
accomplished without
passion."*

Christian Friedrich Hebbel

I sat outside the Grimaldi conference centre in Monte Carlo feasting my eyes upon the Mediterranean Sea. The warm sun of early April was a joy to my skin. I closed my eyes and took a big breath of the sea air and a huge smile radiated and vibrated with a serene energy throughout my whole body. I realized that my greatest passion in life is water. I cannot live without water and when I am near it, it speaks so beautifully to all my cells, nerves, and most of all, to my heart and soul. I feel refreshed, energized, calm, balanced, creative, and in complete harmony with my expansive and beautiful inner spirit.

I was speaking at a conference on the subjects of Life Balancing and Creativity. It was an interesting time in Monte Carlo because it was during the mourning period for the recent death of Prince Rainer. It was as if the entire city was shrouded in black, as all citizens were asked to wear black in respect for His Excellency. My topic of Life Balancing and Creativity seemed uncannily appropriate for the time. In my workshops, one major topic was the question of passion. "What are you passionate about in your life?" or "What are your passions in life?" Monte Carlo was in the midst of ceremony and respect for Rainer and the royal family, and Rainer's passionate legacy that built this tiny principality.

The attendees at the conference were very passionate about their work and what they were doing in their lives. The big question was, Did they realize this? Were they able to say, I am passionate about my profession?

Passion is a very high-energy frequency that moves within and around us. It is the substance that truly motivates, inspires, and drives us. Where does it come from? It comes from a deep place of love in the heart. This energy can move mountains when used and called to action.

When I asked the participants in my workshop to answer the questions about passion, they generally were hard-pressed for answers. I could see the fear in some people's faces, confusion in some, while joy in others.

They deeply questioned themselves to find out, "What am I passionate about?" They even asked, "What is passion?" It was as if I had come from outer space and asked them a totally alien question in a language they didn't understand. I was perplexed by this notion.

I then realized that most of us move through life disconnected to what really makes us spin, buzz, or simply function in life. We are numb to our passions. We are also often taught that they may be frivolous and not important to make a living. In fact, if you combine your passions, or at least part of them, with your livelihood, imagine how exciting that would be.

The word "passion" rarely comes into conversations today because we are so busy about external "stuff." I asked my participants to think about this for a moment, and draw or write down on a piece of paper, what were they passionate about or what were their passions in life.

Once they had drawn or written this down, I asked them to reflect on a time when passion was very present in their lives. Then, when I asked them to share their discoveries, some people said they realized they were in the wrong profession; others decided they wanted to get their passions back in their lives, whether it be through hobbies, sports, crafts, or entertainment, and they began to see what they were passionate about within their profession. This inspired many and motivated them to take action. For some, it was like finding a new purpose in life.

Making space for passion in your life and embracing it gives power to your whole being. It gives you knowledge and confirmation that "yes, I am passionate." Everyone is passionate about something. It just takes going inside—deeply at times—to really discover and be aware of what the passions may be. In fact, they are usually staring you in the face. They are present with you all the time, you just may be moving away from them, instead of toward them.

When you live life according to your passions, sadness seems to melt away. When you honour your passions, you become happier because you are doing what is heartfelt, and this gives you great satisfaction and energy. Suppressing your passions due to your position or situation in life is stifling and draining. Your passions come from a love and heartfelt desire for a purpose in your life. It is, in many ways, about living what and who you really are.

Of course, one needs to address what the passions are and the positive effect they may have not only on you, but also on society as a whole. Some people may be passionate about the darker side of life, such as war or crime. This is not what I am speaking about. I am speaking about balance, harmony, peace, and an overall happiness in your performance as an individual in the community of life.

Along with the participants in my workshops, I reflected upon my own passions in life. I realized that some of my passions were the love for my mother, friends, family; my figure skating, coaching, and choreography for forty years; my health and well-being; and for music, dance, making money, travelling, learning, yoga, meditation, giving speeches, entertaining, and, most of all, my passion for people and assisting them in reaching their potential through the realization of their passions.

As I reviewed my experiences, I could see that I was driven by a variety of factors, but the main factor was passion. I had been driven to succeed as a competitive figure skater; worked with world and Olympic champions; experienced pride through the achievement of others; lived in and travelled to many countries; and gathered a wonderful group of friends. Passion for what I love is my driving force and the underbelly of my courage to act when the going gets tough.

You might say that you don't have so many passions, but I challenge you to look at the different areas of your life and think about what makes you passionate. You can be passionate about a friend, your work, colours, sport, stamp collecting, cooking, public speaking, thinking outside the box, empowering discussions and debates, politics, children, the environment, a good laugh, and the list goes on. Passion is a driving force. When passion is combined with your goals, time seems to disappear, energy abounds, and your heartfelt being shines through.

Begin to live your passions
Now, and
Be present with them.

DISCOVERY

Is it important for you to be passionate about what you do in life? ~ What are you passionate about? ~ Write a list or draw your passions. When you live according to your passions, what does it do for you? ~ When do you want to begin living more passionately?

Pearl • **Practice**

Oyster • **Edmonton, Canada**

"Practice
means to perform,
over and over again in
the face of all obstacles, some
act of vision, of faith, of desire.
Practice is a means of inviting the
perfection desired."

Martha Graham

I was standing on the ice rink one chilly fall morning at the Royal Glenora Club in Edmonton working on some figure skating choreography with a top nationally ranked Canadian skater. We were running through his program doing some last minute touch-ups before we headed off to an international competition in Germany. He was having a few problems with his jumps, his attitude was fairly positive, but I could see that he was not fully trained or practiced for this point in the season.

Normally, I wouldn't get to attend one of these competitions, as his technical coach would accompany him. This time, however, his coach asked me to go in his place. I was delighted to accompany my skater because this would be my last opportunity to do so with him, as he was retiring after the competitive season.

A month before, he had had a most disastrous competition in the US, where he ended up second to last. Consequently, his morale and confidence were very low. It was a challenge to get him motivated for the competition in Germany. His coach and I worked as a team, so we did our best to motivate him.

When you are a honed athlete of this calibre, a poor result in a competition can throw you off and put you out of focus, disorienting you until you can get in the "groove" again. I sensed that the skater was not completely in his "groove" yet, but hoped that he would be able to put his mental power to work in Germany.

On the first day of practice in Germany, I could see that he was having trouble with his jumps. I thought it was due to the jet lag. It was as if all his training and knowledge of his athletic, tuned body was out of balance.

I had to dig deep inside my knowledge, as I had a lot of responsibility to assist him. I had to keep him focused, but his body language and results of practice showed he was just not yet there. We spoke about it, and as the competition day approached, he improved but was still not in top form.

The short program arrived and almost exactly the same thing happened as in the US competition one month earlier. He fell three times on important elements and the performance lacked elegance and focus. Each time he fell, my heart sank and felt the pain going on inside of him as he continued on with courage. I thought, What am I going to say to him to boost his confidence and at the same time be realistic about what he's capable of?

When he came off the ice, he was in disbelief and shock. He couldn't understand what had happened. After a few moments, we chatted about it and devised a plan for moving forward to the long program.

On the day of the long program, his practice was mediocre, but he was digging deep inside himself, as a good competitor would do.

The warm-up before the competition was good and he said he felt en forme. He began his program with gusto and energy. Then he fell, and fell again, again, and again. Each time he stumbled, I couldn't believe it. My heart was reaching out to him. I am sure at some point he felt like simply skating off the ice, as the program was not worth salvaging. After he finished his program, I could see a wounded being coming toward me. The best thing I could do was just be there for him in a quiet way.

We sat down, his head in his hands and my hand on his back. He was in a state of shock and began to cry, which was not like him. Words at this point would be wasted as they wouldn't be heard, but on the other hand the athlete was waiting for my words of wisdom.

I told him this was not the time to begin to analyze this situation, and I suggested we meet the next day to look at this with a broader perspective.

The next day, we went for a long walk before I was to leave Germany. He was still in disbelief and walked in a rather dazed state. We looked at what he had done that season, what he had not done, and what he could do better. He had about eight weeks left to the national championships and to qualify for the Olympic team. He had time to regroup, refocus, and concentrate on his initial goals.

He decided to take a few days off to contemplate his intentions for the next training period. I suggested he sit down and create a training path for the forthcoming weeks. He was to set out mini objectives and goals. He was also to institute a visualization practice to envision what he needed to do, wanted, and how he would move toward that vision. I reassured him that his coach and I would assist and support him emotionally, mentally, physically, and spiritually.

During the next few weeks, I watched his training process and practices change. His confidence was growing and growing. He was committed from the heart to achieve a position on the Olympic team. He was committed to put this "bad" start to the year behind him and move toward the goal. He practiced and practiced, refining his technique, aerobic capacity, and choreography as well as his mental power. We even changed his competitive skating outfits so that he would not have memories of old performances.

One week prior to the Canadian national championships, an interesting turn of events happened to his closest training partner, the then current Canadian and world champion. Due to an injury, he had to drop out of the competition, which left the coveted championship open. The door was opened for my skater, despite the fact that another person was favoured to win.

Even with this fact in mind, he left for the Canadian championships in great shape and with confidence and excitement.

His short program was a success. He performed the best he had all season, which placed him in second position. Then the final long program came. The favoured skater, who was in the first position going into the long program, skated before him and made a couple of mistakes, which the marks reflected.

My skater entered the ice with confidence. His hard-earned training over the past weeks was behind him now; the moment of reckoning was here, and there didn't appear to be any remnants of the earlier season lingering in his mind. He was set to go. He was in the "groove."

He began the long program with confidence and landed one jump after the other like never before. His flow of the skating edge was like silk, his energy was even throughout. The television commentators were blown away about his every move and clean technique; and the crowd became more and more excited as he neared the end of his program. They were on their feet before he ended. The crowd roared and roared.

His performance was amazing to watch. He had the best skate of his whole career. It was an inspired performance that energized the audience and his entire being. No one had ever seen him perform so well.

As he sat in the "kiss and cry area" with his coach next to him awaiting the marks, I sensed the glow of his inner being. He had practiced and practiced and visualized this moment with focus and determination. The marks appeared for the long program, his eyes exploded with joy along with his coaches. This was one of those moments in life which would never ever be repeated again. Then the final results for the whole competition flashed up on the screen and he had won the coveted national championships. This performance and win was the culmination of his career in many ways. The many unexpected turn of events turned, literally, into gold for him.

He returned to Edmonton to a hero's welcome at the airport. Friends, family, TV, press, and his great friend and training partner were all there with lights flashing from their cameras to share this moment of glory. I had never seen him so happy. I was witnessing a changed, inspired, transformed person.

My mind went back to previous weeks when he was about to give everything up and we talked about a new training plan. We realized that when things aren't necessarily going well, how important it is to review and sometimes change direction or strategies. New methods needed to be honestly recognized and implemented.

There was a combination of elements that led to this major turn around; one of them was reaching out for other professional help with a sports psychologist. Another was to review the balance of his mental, physical, emotional, and spiritual capacities. All of the changes were realized by his fierce commitment to focused practice. It goes to show that, with a conscious and committed practice from the heart, miracles can happen. This was his moment of glory, transforming his life from that moment in time.

For each of us, this commitment to practice is what we all can do in our everyday lives, whatever our walk of life, situations, and professions. We are constantly practicing. The question is, "Are we practicing with the right focus, intention, and from the heart?" When we want to change habits and behaviours in our life, it takes a conscious practice to create our desired results. It is truly a re-learning that can only be done through practice of new behaviours or procedures.

Commit to practicing with consciousness and awareness, it will add value to your life, and to others around you.

DISCOVERY

Have you ever thought about life as one practice after the other? ~ We are practicing something all the time. The question is, what is your driving force? ~ What is practice to you? ~ What are some of the results of your practice? ~ What can a well-focused and committed practice do for your performance in life?

21st Pearl

Pearl • **Consistency**

Oyster • **Paris, France**

"I
pray to be like
the ocean, with soft
currents, maybe waves at
times. More and more, I want the
consistency rather than the highs
and the lows."

DREW BARRYMORE

This story originated in New York City at Sky Rink, where I was teaching skating at that beautiful ice rink high atop the city on the sixteenth floor.

In those days I wore flamboyant clothes, bright colours and pushed the boundaries of The Skating Club of New York, a rather conservative organization. It had been a stuffy, upper-crust club for many years and was now slowly becoming more liberal.

One of my clients was a lovely actress. We would dance around the rink with great abandon and enjoy each other's company. She was simply charming and full of laughs. She had a daughter who I also taught and partnered through her Gold dance tests (the highest tests in those days). Her daughter was also a budding actress.

One day, I asked my client what she thought were her daughter's chances in the "biz." She said that she wasn't "consistent" enough. My head tilted a bit to think about her comment. She recognized this tilt and before I said anything, she said, "I don't mean just showing up on time or learning your lines or being persistent, but rather having a spirited consistency in performance, behaviour, and focus." Now, I realize more mindfully what she was referring to—consistently performing in life from the inner spirit.

This pearl stuck to me and has ever since. It keeps popping up in my life and the meaning continues to resonate on a deeper level. How could I become as consistent as a dancer? I struggled with understanding the practice of consistency. Of course at that time, 1980, I didn't really grasp the concept at all. But then I turned my primary focus to developing a physical, mental, and emotional consistency.

Not long after this conversation, a friend who was dancing in Paris persuaded me to come to dance there. I thought it was a great idea to go to the home of cabaret and learn consistency. I wanted to develop consistency so that it became part of my muscle memory, my cellular level, and my spirit. There is a saying that until knowledge enters the muscle it is only a rumour; this statement is also speaking about the spiritual muscle.

Upon my arrival in Paris, my friend told me that the Bal du Moulin Rouge was looking for dancers. The infamous Moulin Rouge dance hall, the Toulouse-Lautrec joint, the former brothel. It was so full of history; I could feel it as I walked into the theatre. If only the walls could speak! I instantly fell in love with it and the dancers were a lot of fun. I got the job quite easily and proceeded to dance my body through two shows a night for nearly six months.

Bus-loads of tourists would come to the Moulin Rouge twice a night, not only for the glamour of the costumes, lights, dancing, singing, and the bare-breasted girls, but also for the famous cancan. This was always a tremendous event to behold as the cancan girls jumped and flew through the air before landing in the splits. Then they would get up and do it again, over and over. Punishment, I say. Luckily for the guys, they simply had to do multiple kicks and lift the girls, which was not always that easy. This is how my awareness of consistency really kicked in—no pun intended.

When I began at the Moulin, I wanted to experience the spirit of the show, but most of all, my intentions were for performing, consistently performing at my maximum twice every night. For the entire time I was there, I checked in at the stage door and warm-up way before any of the other male dancers would. As I sprawled over the floor to stretch, the girls would enter and climb over or walk around me to the change area on their way to their dressing rooms. It went something like this …

Check-in, 9:15 p.m.,
stretch,
makeup,
perform,

touch up makeup,
perform,
shower,
check-out, 2:30 a.m.

I worked very hard at the Moulin and performed on a consistent basis, while it seemed the other dancers who had been there for many months or years had fallen into autopilot mode. I was the "raw meat" still learning the ropes. They often joked with me about how dedicated I was, and wondered how long it would take for me to go on autopilot by simply arriving late, quickly slapping on the makeup, and running out on stage just in time. They had already developed their muscle memory, I suppose, and perhaps now took it for granted. I didn't want to become like this at all.

Little by little, each day in Paris I was accomplishing my goal to learn what my Sky Rink client had talked about. I wanted this in my muscle memory so badly. I kept hearing her words. They buzzed in my head, especially when I got very tired of performing. But because of my commitment to consistency, I could be relied upon to give my best performance every show instead of simply "marking it," going through the motions. I told myself many times when I was exhausted or depressed during those late nights, "Consistency, not complacency."

I have now come to understand consistency has a much deeper meaning; it leads to a behaviour, a spiritual behaviour. Consistency comes from the inside, and the outside is a manifestation of how you honour this behaviour, your performance in life and spirit. It is first, part of the spirit, a steady entity that is always there, always honoured if you tap into it. It is also free. It can be spontaneous as well. It is physical, having memory of your physical movements and activities. It is mentally intelligent. It can also be emotional. It adds value to your life and others, because your consistent performance or behaviour can be relied upon, trusted. It will be felt and noticed internally by you, and externally by others.

Before we performed the second cancan of the night at nearly two a.m., I could be found warming up in a sort of half-sleep phase, but still remembering my goal. Often, I felt like saying to hell with this goal when I was exhausted and thought, What normal person would be doing the cancan at this time of night? Then, I realized how lucky I was to be one of a handful of people in the world doing this. That thought was exciting enough and would always spur me on.

After months of being dedicated
I came out with consistency.
My goal was reached.
How did I know?
Every time I danced or performed afterward,
no matter the technique
or
choreography,
my body,
mind, heart,
and soul
would jump
into my deep
muscle memory.
It became Knowledge
and was
not Rumour anymore.
Consistency had now taken up

Residency
within me
on a very Deep Level.
A learned value
was
NOW
part of
my Being.

Consistency is necessary in all parts of our lives. It is there hiding in the wings, waiting to sprout forth—ready and willing to participate whenever called upon. Some people perhaps don't find it necessary in their life to call up this value, that is okay, or maybe they refer to it as something else.

Developing consistency takes conscious effort, courage, and the ability to change. Awaken it from the subconscious. When you set out to learn this value you are beginning to create the muscle memory that recognizes one level of consistency. When you consistently move or live from the spirit, the mind, body, heart, and soul become a holistic muscle. Yes, you can be consistent physically, mentally, emotionally, and spiritually, but if you separate them, you lose the full energy and wisdom of consistency. It will be felt and noticed internally by you and externally by others. There can be no separation if you wish to live in consistent harmony with your speech, communication, projects, relationships, play, and however you wish to participate in life.

Move toward developing your consistency muscle each day. You will reap the rewards in life and perhaps you to can do your own version of the cancan one day!

DISCOVERY

What is consistency to you? ~ Is consistency important at all for your life? ~ Have you ever thought about consistency in the various components that make up your life? ~ What type of effort do you put behind your actions in life that can build up consistency? ~ How would you further benefit from a practice of consistency?

Pearl • **Patience**

Oyster • **Kerala, India**

*"Patience
is the companion of
wisdom."*

SAINT AUGUSTINE

I had just finished standing on my head and it seemed all the blood in my body had rushed into it, when at that very moment, an *Aha* moment of patience appeared in my mind.

I had arrived at Mumbai airport in India late, under a star-filled night. Something inside of me glowed with serenity and a voice inside me said, "You are home." Impressions began to flow inside of me like a river. The odours and smells that floated on the gentle night breeze seemed offensive yet familiar in a peculiar way. The sounds of beeping horns from taxis, cars, and the like, and the sights of cows on the street, no street signs, and so much more seemed familiar. I was to come to realize something greater, and that was being present to the power of patience.

On New Year's Eve, I took a train trip from Kollam station in Kerala to Kochi with a friend named Gopi. It would be my debut trip on an Indian train. Gopi went off to buy the train tickets for us while I waited on the train platform. The platform was full of women in colourful saris with their husbands and children, and male students in their late teens and early twenties, lugging many suitcases and bags, or one very old suitcase.

The December sun was hot, humidity was high, and there were crowds of people; however, the platform was relatively quiet. The gentle wind seemed to calm people as they moved at a languid pace. This calm I sensed with such clarity.

Gopi returned with tickets for second-class seats. From my experience, I knew our seats would be a bit hard on my tender Western bottom; for those who have never had the pleasure of riding the Indian railways, this is definitely an adventure to be experienced.

As the train noisily pulled into the station, the platform rapidly came to life. The people began to jockey for positions, push, shove, talk louder, and eventually yell at times. The physical push to get onto the train was an event unto itself. Once on board, Gopi and I found ourselves without seats and standing at the end of our train car sandwiched between other travellers.

In India, it appears no one is ever "alone"—well, this sandwich was going to continue for the next five hours on a very slow train to Kochi. I glanced over at Gopi and he had gracefully settled in with the others, accepting our fate for the trip. I was a bit perturbed and a little confused: How could I hang in there for five hours? What was this fate I had got myself into? Do I hold onto my wallet, which I can't reach, my bags, what do I do? "Get used to it" sprang to my mind. "You're here now and there seemed to be no way out."

This was definitely no luxury, high-speed TGV. As I stood, I knew I would never fall down if the train suddenly jolted or stopped as many other bodies buffered me. This situation was not for the claustrophobic. There we were, with people hanging out of the train doors, on the outsides of the trains, with windows wide open with bars on them, and every space possible occupied by a body or luggage. The sandwich was packed full of ingredients.

As we moved along to the clippity-clap of the train rattling in my ears and soul, I began to notice that hardly anyone was now talking. Calm really settled in, I sensed this must be what being in the present is truly about. Overriding that thought was also how patient these people were. Maybe being patient and present is the same thing, I thought.

I tried to move myself and change position but could only do so if others around me shifted a little. It was kind of like a slow-motion choreographed dance. I glanced into dark glassy eyes of the people next to me and also in those in other compartments. Often, smiles would return. Women were holding sleeping children. Men were gazing in the distance. The tempo of people's breathing was legato. Life seemed to have come to a standstill. I marvelled at this sense of calm and clarity amidst the seeming chaos.

As I continued to look around and catch the eye of those near me, I felt as though I was watching a group meditation. They had all gone into trance-like states. The whole energy of the car was tranquil, soft, and gentle as the breeze. Through osmosis, I felt this was also happening to me.

All of a sudden, the word "patience" popped into my mind; how patient these people were as we slowly travelled 120 kilometres in five hours. Patience. The frustration and annoyance that usually goes through an impatient Westerner's mind at this point would normally be unbearable to be around. In opposition to the Indian's response, I am sure the inner dialogue of a Westerner would go something like this: "Why is this taking so long? Bloody train. Can't they get it together? All these people, what's wrong with them?" I am sure one could go on forever, creating more and more anxiety.

Instead of heading into my anxious inner dialogue, I became curious. I tuned in to my breathing. It became slower and slower till I was in an active yoga state of meditation, creating a union with my surroundings.

What were the inner dialogues of these people? Their exteriors showed nothing. They seemed at peace, tranquil, and meditative, and most of all, seemingly present to the here and now and no more. They were patient, realizing that reacting would do no good at all. They were totally in the moment. They had surrendered to the fact they would not reach their destination any easier or faster by being aggressive or impatient. This would be their karma, destiny for this very moment in time. It was mine as well.

As the train approached Kochi, the calm surroundings drastically changed as people jockeyed for positions to exit the train. People began to push harder as the train neared the station. I became a little frightened and wondered if this is what it would feel like to be stampeded to death. I was afraid to be separated from Gopi. It was a scary reality after such penetrating calm. What a paradox. That, in many ways, defines

India—a paradox.

Loud talking and yelling began to erupt, disrupting the quiet just moments before. People threw their luggage off the train as it meandered into the station. Some jumped off the moving train and others waited till it stopped. I asked myself, "Was this patience or stillness actually a façade, or was it reality? Was it a silent bomb in the waiting?" Maybe so, but I got the sense that patience is really about honouring the here and now. Being in the moment.

Once the train did come to a final resting stop, those wanting to get on at the same time confronted the hubbub of people exiting. This happened with a fair amount of shoving, pushing, and noise. It was like taking apart a clubhouse sandwich and then rebuilding it again with new flavours and tastes.

As the Indians on the train became impatient on arrival in Kochi, once off the train, they rapidly went back to being part of a patient surrounding. There was absolutely no dwelling on what had just happened. It was being one with the moment.

Once I was out of the masses, calm came over me again. I could see from Gopi that this whole event didn't faze him one bit. Through him and everyone else, I realized how much "in the now" and present everyone was—or, at least, it seemed to be so.

Patience exists within us all at all times. It is a practice, a study, and a reflection of our interior life. It is sitting, pulsating, and a living entity of everyone. This was evident from my train trip. Impatience is a response to something, someone, or ourselves, such as an anxiety we have built up in our minds.

The surrendering of the people, as well as myself, to the now, took away any anxiety felt from the impatience with the train, its speed, crowds of people, and claustrophobic situation. This was all gone. I was listening and learning from my chosen experience.

Our patience is being tested every moment of the day. Patience is action in full force and is turned on all of the time, if we tune into its rhythm. See, feel, and be one, in the now, with patience. Eventually the external environment will cease its clamour and our inner dialogue will quieten to a gentle roar, like the sound of the rolling surf. Here is where the learning begins. This awakening is opening up to the presence of patience.

I later realized we must have patience in order to learn how to stand on our heads!

DISCOVERY

Think of a time when you were very patient. What did this feel like? ~ What was going through your mind, body, and spirit? ~ How different is this to when you are impatient? ~ What does patience do for you in life? ~ What are some ways that you can begin to create this on an ongoing basis? ~ Patience is definitely a virtue.

23rd Pearl

Pearl • **Silence**

Oyster • **Ganeshpuri, India**

*"We
need to find God,
and he cannot be found
in noise and restlessness. God
is the friend of silence. See how
nature—trees, flowers, grass—grows
in silence; see the stars, the moon
and the sun, how they move in silence
... We need silence to be able to touch
souls."*

MOTHER TERESA

I had the opportunity to spend three blissful weeks at a meditation ashram in Ganeshpuri, India. The ashram is situated in a very poor region of Maharashtra State in the Tamsa Valley, about two hours north of Mumbai.

On my way to the ashram, I noticed the vegetation was dry, many gnarled trees framed the road, and the villages we passed through were very poor. Sacred cows wandered freely with the goats and dogs on the sides of the roads. As I approached the ashram, the vegetation changed to lush green behind a big fence.

I felt as though I had left reality and moved into heaven on earth. It was a rich oasis of beauty, serenity, and stillness. This was what I was searching for at this point in my life. I sensed a beautiful glow come over my body, inside and out, and during my stay there, that glow became warmer and deeper.

The retreat involved a ten-day practice of complete silence. There would be no speaking, only gesturing. If we were in extreme desperation to communicate, only then could we talk. We could however, chant if we wished. I wondered how could I do this for one day let alone ten days. Many of my fellow silent retreat participants also expressed the same uncertainty. I asked myself, why would I want to even participate in this practice? Are we ever silent in our normal day-to-day lives? So, why should I practice something that seemed like harsh penance? Yet, it was my choice to do this, so I wholeheartedly jumped into the practice, absorbing all the moments within the silence and comparing them to non-silence.

The first day of silence was a challenge, but I survived without any problems. The second and third days were even more challenging and frustrating, both mentally and physically. It is kind of like learning to walk or ride a bike for the first time. After four days, I found myself completely surrendering to the practice.

My days were defined by a clear routine. I would wake at 3:30 a.m. in the depth of the pitch-black night. I proceeded to my meditation practice with my fellow participants. When meditation was completed, we would chant. After this, I would take an early morning walk around and around the "field of dreams." That was my name for this magnificent, huge green space. There, I would stop to watch the sunrise, do my yoga exercises, and feast on the early morning fragrance of the many tropical flowers. Breakfast was silent and it was a time to actually indulge in cherishing every morsel of my food. It tasted so good when I focused on the savoury flavours.

During the day, we would have classes on yogic philosophy, more meditation, chanting, and in the afternoon, we would do "seva," selfless service. Seva was comprised of cleaning, gardening, doing dishes, and various other activities, all in silence, so we could focus on the moment, every movement, of the activity. In the high heat of the afternoon, I would take a nap. Later in the day, I would read in the gardens, chant and meditate some more, eat dinner, and prepare for bed at 8:30 p.m.

I found that every sound I heard, every scent I smelled, and every taste I tasted became more accentuated as the days went on. My sight focused on things I may never have looked at before, my senses opened up more and more each day, awakening new discoveries not only externally, but internally as well. I began to just "be" with others, my environment, and myself.

Luckily, everyone in the ashram supported the participants of the silent retreat. No one spoke to us and silence was maintained everywhere.

As the days progressed, I observed the people around me. Many of them would avoid the gaze of another person, but some would stare into your eyes and smile from the heart. That smile seemed to come from a deeper place each day. For some people, the agony was intense and you could see this from their body movement. Perhaps, more discoveries were going on inside of them, and silence was intensifying the experience. There was a total freedom of movement as we ate, meditated, chanted, exercised, and walked the grounds.

For me, I sensed a growing calmness each day throughout my entire body. The constant chatter inside of my head was being replaced by silence. I felt as though there was a clearing of the cobwebs that had been clogging my mind, body, and soul. I felt as though I was lowering the activity from my mind, letting it sink toward the centre of my body, my navel. The sensation felt holistic, natural. By cutting out the chatter of my everyday discursive thought patterns, I was able to reach deeper to the source of the Self. I was living from my whole body, not just from my head.

As we sank further,
Our faces became brighter and softer,
Eyes warmer and
More defined,
And our whole bodies were
Completely smiling,
Inside and out.
Ah, the total physical smile.
The chatter disappeared
And left only the important
Pieces of information.
It was as if someone pressed
Delete.
This is a breath of fresh air
And what we were searching for
Is
Silence.

At the end of the retreat, we were given the choice to release our vow of silence or to continue with a practice of silence. It would be a challenge to speak again. It would be as if I had to get my voice up and running again after such lack of use. The words would seem uncomfortable and slightly foreign. Before making our decisions, I saw some people felt very uncomfortable about speaking and wanted to continue, as they were not finished yet with their quest.

Personally, I wanted to simply stay in silence, as it was comforting. The biggest realization for most of us was how much drivel we speak about in life. We do talk such nonsense most of the time. It is not necessary.

I wondered why we talk so much. Perhaps we chatter incessantly due to our insecurity, our need to be heard, and our self-important and egotistical nature constantly demanding centre stage. In actuality, many of us are filled with fear when conversations are momentarily silent. It is a challenge not to speak, but it took me closer to the Self and removed the dreadful, chattering gremlins that get in the way of reaching my potential.

I wondered how I could retain this state after I left this haven of serenity. I knew I would be once again constantly speaking in reaction to the numerous external distractions and influences surrounding me. The list seems endless: work, telephones, friends and family, the media, and countless others. All of this can be destabilizing and unbalancing. However, with this experience, I became aware of another way of being, and with different practices that I learned, I would be able to call up this spiritual muscle memory again and again.

Silence surrounds you and
Is at your fingers tips
Every moment of the Day.

It is your choice to take or leave.
Give yourself a fully engaged chance
To be at your fullest potential.
Silence assists this.
Take a deep breath
Between the sequences
Of your speech.
Take a few moments
Every Day
To
Be
Silent
And
Not Speak.
The calmness that reigns is
Like a beautiful lotus
Floating
On
The
Water.

Silence tunes you into
The senses and everything
Around you becomes a
Peak experience.
So,
See,
Hear,
Feel,
Touch,

Smell,
And sense the
Inner voice of
The intuition.

Join me NOW in this reflection,
Take a deep breath
And just
Surrender to the silence.
Be one with it.
Flow NOW.

As I drove away from the ashram, I looked back and saw friends waving with big warm smiles that emanated from their whole bodies. Silence was within them and seemed to be with me as well. As I sat in the car, I observed the little Indian children riding bikes two or three times their size. When our silent eyes met, we smiled, loud as could be. I saw the vegetation, dry grass, and the trees, all with a veneer of silence around them. Suddenly, the "real" world intruded for the first time in many days, as I received a text message on my mobile phone. I smiled and decided to answer it later, and I continued to gaze out the car window, holding the glow of silence within me as I observed the activity all around.

DISCOVERY

Where you do find silence in your life? ~ What happens to your mind, body, and soul when you are practicing silence? ~ How can creating an inner world of silence assist you in the different aspects of your life? ~ Silence is a key to the powerful source of energy that radiates within you.

24TH PEARL

Pearl • **Surrender**

Oyster • **Edmonton, Canada**

*"The
river runs through
you, expect when it
doesn't."*

DR STEPHEN GILLIGAN

I was living in London, England, licking my wounds from working with a friend on a failed Internet venture. We had a great idea, but we were at the end of the Internet start-up boom and well into the decline of the "IT empire," as it was then referred to.

What was I going to do? Money was short; I was feeling unsettled and a bit depressed. Out of the blue, came a call for applications for the director of ceremonies job of the 8th IAAF World Championships in Athletics in Edmonton 2001. I thought it sounded interesting, accepted the challenge, and surrendered to the opportunity.

Ah, surrender. I must admit that the word "surrender" really didn't come into my vocabulary until after 1995, when I began meditating. However, "letting go" had been familiar to me, and often in my life, I would hear others say, "Just let go." It didn't have much meaning to me back then—or so I thought. This is a story of the pearl of surrender, and the balance between holding too tight or too loose.

To my surprise, within a few weeks of submitting my application, the producer called. I found out he was someone I had worked with on the 1988 Winter Olympic Games ceremonies in Calgary. He said he would like to conduct an interview with the selection committee, as I had been shortlisted to one of three applicants. I was excited and told him he could call me in Barcelona, where I was going to spend my remaining days in Europe before returning to Canada.

The first interview went well. I was then invited to Edmonton for a final in-person interview. The final interview flowed, just like a river. We were gently bouncing off of each other's questions and answers, letting the flow take us on the journey. I felt as if I had surrendered myself not only to the situation, but also to my spirit and my heart. I was moving from a different place within me.

This interview seemed to take a very different path and intention than previous interviews in my life. Normally at a final interview, I would put lots of pressure on myself and construct numerous expectations in my head. I would get extremely creative as well as nervous. My mind would go into overtime mode, imagining myself having the job and how wonderful it would be. This would lead me to exert pressure on myself, as well as getting "too tight," about the outcome. But this time seemed different.

En route to my interview that day, I had been listening to someone on the radio speaking about "Buffalo Runners." Buffalo Runners are part of the history of the First Nations people of the Canadian prairies. They were young boys who were chosen for their speed, agility, intelligence, and bravery to herd the buffalo toward a cliff. The buffalo would then fall over the cliff to their death. Near the bottom of the cliff, camp was set up to skin, cure, and feast on the hunt. I came to realize these Buffalo Runners needed to fully surrender to their souls to perform this honoured role. They could not be "too tight" or "too loose" in their thoughts and actions, otherwise, their survival walked a tenuous line. There seemed to be a very strong relationship between surrendering, or letting go, and the Buffalo Runners' quest.

This information was serendipitous. Perhaps this was a good omen or perhaps simply a good metaphor for life. In my mind, I thought this could be a seed for the creation of the opening ceremonies of The World's. I was listening, observing, as well as surrendering to my surroundings and situation. I gratefully absorbed these ideas. Perhaps, I was given this message as inspiration for my interview; it at least offered some creative ammunition.

The final interview went very well. I was not too tight and not too loose. My energy was balanced and I spoke from my heart with playfulness, confidence, and strength. I even had the chance to slide in my seed of the Buffalo Runners, which received generous positive feedback.

Within a few weeks I had the job, signed the contract, and was off to Edmonton to begin the creative process with my seed firmly in my back pocket. I was now running with the buffalo to see where we would end up.

I sense that surrender played a large role in me winning the contract for this position. I somehow completely surrendered to this project without me actually thinking about it. There was great timing and flow that also surrounded the interview; it was working with me not against me.

Dr Stephen Gilligan, a renowned and respected hypnotherapist, speaks about being not too tight and not too loose. He suggests "too tight" is fundamentalist (thinking and acting like that there is only one way) and "too loose" is commercialist (no structure, anything goes, sloppy). The surrender is the balance point between those opposing points, and that is where I was at mentally and spiritually when I got the job.

For the creative process, I persistently indulged myself on a not too tight and not too loose basis. It seemed I was working from a balanced, confident place in my heart. I listened and felt its flow.

A Buffalo Runner has to surrender himself to his inner and outer environments. He needs to be brave, intelligent, and flexible to shift course at a split second. He needs to be aware of himself, his actions, and where he is going. In the heat of the action he needs to be fully aware internally and externally. He needs to be fully alert and focused on the job intended. He also needs to surrender to himself, his senses, and gracefully move with the flow. If the Buffalo Runner totally gave himself up to the buffalo and the elements, he would be lost, perhaps forever.

Surrendering is definitively not about giving up, as some may think. It is intelligently committing to action with the right amount of effort. It is trusting in an awakened spirit.

By surrendering to the "not too tight" and "not too loose" concept, we buoyantly balance ourselves in a powerful way. Everyone becomes a winner, empowered, strong, and confident.

Surrender to the river of life and you will be supported with grace. When I apply this principle to my story, I can see how smoothly and gracefully the process went along, I sensed I moved with just the right amount of energy and focus. The rest was in someone else's hands.

When I reflect upon some of my stressful moments in life, I can see my unsuccessful approaches were perhaps closer to the extremes of "too tight" or "too loose." It takes practice and awareness to manage surrendering. It is a challenge, but a worthwhile one, helping to preserve both sanity and health.

The story of the Buffalo Runners became the seed that grew into a major tree for both the opening and closing ceremonies of The World's. In fact, everyone on the creative team surrendered to creating the first production number of the opening ceremonies as a contemporary adaptation of Buffalo Running. It turned out to be a very powerful and successful moment.

There were times in Edmonton when I applied way too much pressure on the project, resulting in some very bad feelings and decisions. I realize now they were also a consequence of not applying the right amount of pressure or tension. I am not happy about those situations; however, I have learned that surrendering, being awake, and applying just the right amount of energy can create happiness and well being for all.

I did not consciously realize how much I had surrendered to the project until it was over. It is often the case in life that realizations do not occur when you are caught up in the swirl of life, so to speak. It takes stepping back, reflection, and open observation.

My six months in Edmonton was a brilliant time. I surrendered with all my heart to the process, and it supported me and everyone else with the buoyancy of a vast ocean.

When the buffalo begin
To run.
Surrender
To your soul,
Move with them,
Dance around them, or
Even get out of the way. But
Be Alert,
Flexible,
Focused,
And Balance
The Energy of
"Not too tight,"
And
"Not too loose."
Just take a moment
To
Breathe,
Expand,
And
Surrender
With a Courageous Smile
In your Heart.

DISCOVERY

Have you ever thought about surrender, and what this means to you? ~ Take a moment to think of a situation in your life when you were applying either "too tight" or "too loose" pressure. What were the effects? ~ What would you do now if you were to surrender to the situation in a more open, flexible, and brave way? ~ Be like the Buffalo Runner or the river and surrender internally and externally; find your balance, now.

25TH PEARL

Pearl • **Expansion**

Oyster • **Head-Smashed-In Buffalo Jump, Canada**

"Ever
since I was a
child, I have had this
instinctive urge for expansion
and growth. To me, the function
and duty of a quality human being is
the sincere and honest development of
one's potential."

Bruce Lee

Recently, I was taking a neuro-linguistic programming (NLP) workshop. In one of the exercises, I needed to recall from memory a very high energetic state of being. This was to create a desired state that I wanted when presenting to an audience. In my minds eye, up popped an experience which was one of the most profound in my life. As I reflected on it, the word "expansion" came into my heart and soul.

I was driving to Head-Smashed-In Buffalo Jump in southern Alberta, Canada on a dry hot summer's day. As I drove south from Calgary toward the foothills of the Rockies, the flat plains seemed to extend gracefully forever. My vision seemed to expand forever and the sky was big, very, very big. Everyone should experience this place once in his or her life; it is God's country.

As I drove, the golden grassy fields on either side of the highway swayed in the gentle, calming breeze. With my window rolled down and arm resting on the open window frame, my mind wandered back to the forefathers of this land of the Plains Indians, the Blackfoot Nation. Historically, this is where they made their home and still do today. It is as if you can taste the history, as well as sense their spirits permeating the elements. Ahh, what bliss!

It seemed as though I had been driving forever through this exquisite landscape. My breathing slowed down and reached deeper into my body, to the depths of my soul. I felt at peace and in harmony with the world and my surroundings. I felt like I was the only person in the world surrounded by open space.

I was getting closer to the foothills of the Rockies. The flat land began to roll and reach higher. Some of the edges of the hills looked like the soft fur of a baby animal. I could see the Head-Smashed-In Buffalo Jump bluff not far in the distance. As I got closer, the majesty of this bluff swept me away.

Built inside of the bluff is Head-Smashed-In Buffalo Jump's

interpretive centre, where one can learn about the history of the area.

As I mentioned in the previous chapter, according to history, the buffalo were herded by Buffalo Runners to the edge of the bluff. The buffalo would stampede off the cliff and fall to their death. At the bottom of the bluff, the Indians would skin and tan the hides, cure the meat for winter, and feast upon their hunt.

I took the elevator to the top of the centre. I exited to the lookout on top of the bluff. The heat of the day caressed my face, my body, and my soul. I was the only person at the lookout. I walked to the edge of the bluff. It was a breathtaking experience. All I could see in front of me was land, land, and more land. I got the sense that perhaps the earth was really flat. I don't believe I have seen anything more beautiful, graceful, and full of human spirit.

I let my eyes slowly scan the horizon, and all I saw was swaying golden grass. I didn't see a person, a building, nothing at all. But what I did see was a sky that reached so wide and so far to the edges of the land. I turned 360 degrees slowly with my arms outstretched. What I saw was more of the same. Flat land laid like a fine woven carpet, rolling hills, mountains in the distance, and sky. I stood totally awestruck with a serene smile upon my lips.

As I inhaled the hot dry air, I realized that this is expansion. I felt the complete expansion of my mind, body, heart, and soul. Not only was I seeing a physical, environmental expansion, but I also realized I could expand my inner being this far as well. I could grab hold of this expanded state, live with it as my inner environment, and recreate it when in a restricted state of being, for a freer perspective and purpose.

During the NLP exercise, this expansion memory appeared. I really felt as if I was in that state of expansion and bliss at Buffalo Jump once again. I could feel the soft, gentle, dry hot wind against my skin, my face and my clothes.

Once I had recreated this state, I began to visualize an upcoming presentation I was to give at a conference. I imagined myself standing on top of the bluff, looking out at the horizon, and I filled this expansive space (environment) with people. I felt open, I felt free, and I felt at one with the people. I didn't feel or act as if I was in a confined physical space, rather the opposite, an expanded space. My words flowed from my heart on the hot gentle breeze toward the audience's ears. They embraced what I had to say and left feeling fulfilled. That was my visualization.

When I stood before the real audience, I again brought back my visualized expanded state. What a feeling that was! It was truly the best presentation I have given. I am grateful for this moment I spent at Head-Smashed-In Buffalo Jump. I will keep this expansion with me forever. I will recall it whenever I begin to feel contracted in my thoughts, business, and most of all, in my vision of life.

Expand into your world,
Expand into the world,
Expand the dome that surrounds you,
Expand into the bigger picture of life.
Stand on the bluff and look at the horizon.
What do you see, What do you feel,
What do you hear, What do you taste,
What do you smell, What do you touch, and
What does your inner most soul say to you?
Expand and let the spirits of the plains guide you
To the Big Space.

DISCOVERY

What is expansion to you? ~ What do you sense when you are in an expanded frame of being? ~ Go inside yourself and really sense the feelings. What is your inner voice saying to you now? ~ Sense the big space within you—it is magical.

Pearl • **Seva**

Oyster • **Tamsa Valley, India**

*"When
you do seva with
love, love is what you
experience."*

SWAMI CHIDVILASANDA

The Tamsa Valley is a very poor and arid area in Maharashtra State, India. It is very close to Ganeshpuri and is full of little villages. The people in this area do not have a lot of possessions or money and rely heavily upon the assistance of philanthropic people and groups for their basic survival.

I had just spent three weeks at a meditation and yoga retreat in Ganeshpuri. A great opportunity was presented to me to spend a morning delivering fortified milk to children in several villages in the area. I thought it would be a great way to end a most inner searching and blissful time. It is my honour to share with you this experience that opened my eyes to the wealth of "seva."

Seva is the practice of performing selfless service, without any expectations or financial rewards. It comes directly from the heart and is a state of pure giving. The reward is selfless and full of love.

The chilly morning I was to do my seva, I woke at 3:30 a.m. to chant and meditate before eating breakfast. After breakfast, I headed to the Foundations compound, where we loaded up the truck with large milk canisters. The driver's deep brown eyes were full of peace, energy, and smiles. I sensed I was in for a real experience.

The driver headed off into the valley over dusty rocky roads. The vegetation was bleak and the trees looked dry but had green foliage. As the truck rocked back and forth, I listened to the milk swishing around in the canisters.

As I looked out the window at the landscape, my mind wandered to my destination. What am I going to see? Will I see deformed, unhealthy, crying, weak children? What was the true gift of this seva I was about to experience? I had no idea, but I was so excited to freely offer myself to the service of others this simple morning in India.

To give from the heart.
To give without any expectations.
To give with love.
To be open to this experience.
To be free in my selfless service,
my seva opportunity.

As we approached the first village, the driver honked his horn several times. What happened next amazed me. I saw little, barefoot children running on the rocky earth from all directions toward us, joyfully yelling and screaming. They wore a variety of donated clothing from the West. It was so funny to see little children with their big dark eyes staring at you with a toque on their head, sweaters with English writing on them, frilly colourful party dresses, pants too big for petite bodies, and so forth. It was a heart-warming site to see.

When the truck came to a stop in front of a little building, the children gathered around the truck welcoming us with open arms. They knew it was milk day. The volunteers, driver, and I poured some of the milk from the large canisters into a bucket. The children lined up with their cups in hand. The oldest children in the bunch would keep the children in line, and assist the very smallest kids. The parents were nowhere to be seen.

My job was to assist pouring the milk into the children's cups. As I poured each cup, I felt I was performing a religious ritual, not unlike the service of Holy Eucharist in Christian tradition. The joy I felt from looking into the eyes of each little child is hard for me to explain. I sensed I was able to see right into their hearts. I realized how appreciative they were of getting this one glass of milk per day. They knew how important it was and how God was providing for them. It was a site to experience and behold. The experience really went to the centre of my soul. My seva was rich with a grace I'd rarely experienced in my life.

After all the children received their milk, they sat down in rows on either concrete or dirt. They put the cup of milk down beside them. While their hands were folded in a prayer position, the driver (or an older boy or girl from the village) would conduct a prayer of thanks and chant, and all the children joined singing the mantra. I could see this would be an added honour for the boy or girl to do this seva ceremony of thanks.

The older children would then assist their youngest siblings to drink their cup of milk. They drank the milk with joy. You could hear a pin drop as they drank. Such a pure innocent spirit filled their little bodies and big hearts. It was so sweet to see their beautiful brown faces smile with milk around their lips. Some children would hope to get another glass of milk, but we were instructed to give only one glass of milk to be equal to all.

We then got back into the truck while the children laughed, smiled, and waved with their cups in hand, and we drove off to our next destination.

We went to a variety of villages giving milk, and the same process happened each time. The truck horn announced to the village and all the little barefoot children would come running. I felt, as I went from one village to the next, my smile getting bigger and wider. My heart became happier and happier. I felt more and more pure love for these little children. I reflected upon how happy they were with the simplest yet one of the most important aspects of their physical survival. Yes, this would seem "simple" to me, coming from the West and land of plenty, but it was truly monumental to them. I was becoming more filled with love as my seva progressed.

One of the greatest teachings for me was that these young people were not poor in spirit, but they were all so rich, healthy, and full of love. They were honoured to have this one glass of fortified milk. They were honoured to have the hand-me-down clothing. That was all they knew and they were so happy.

By the end of the morning, we had visited about twelve villages. As we returned to the compound, I was filled with love and with my seva. I was thankful to give my time and service selflessly to this specific learning opportunity. I realized that giving selflessly brings back so much to the soul and opens our hearts and spirit wider. It reaches deep inside of us to our core.

After I left the truck, the hot sun was not only beating down from the outside, but also the sun and fire inside of me was radiant and full of warmth. This is what seva can bring. We have to get out of the way and just be ourselves, embracing others or situations without any expectations.

It is amazing what a glass of milk can mean. These children's faces are forevermore etched in my mind, body, heart, and soul. Truly, from my heart, I offer my seva, the wisdom of "namaste":

"I honour the divine in you, I honour the divine in me."

DISCOVERY

Do you volunteer or serve? ~ What type of "seva" do you do? ~ What does this give you? Where does it touch you in your soul? ~ Draw a picture of how it makes you feel. Giving and receiving is full of gratitude and grace.

Pearl • **Truth**

Oyster • **Brussels, Belgium**

"Believe
nothing just
because a so-called wise
person said it. Believe nothing
just because a belief is generally
held. Believe nothing just because
it is said in ancient books. Believe
nothing just because it is said to be
of divine origin. Believe nothing just
because someone else believes it.
Believe only what you yourself test
and judge to be true."

BUDDHA

I woke at four a.m. on January 5th, 2005 to write my first Toastmasters speech, "The Icebreaker." This inaugural speech is designed to tell the audience a little about your life and who you are. I sensed my speech was moving through my mind, body, and soul at this very early hour. As I lay in bed, it seemed as if an inner voice was reciting the speech to me. It was about truth. It was about my life to date. Because it was so early in the morning, I thought that perhaps I should just fall back to sleep. No, I thought, here was a great opportunity being presented to me, take it now or it may disappear within the next second. So, off I went to write.

I set the scene. I lit a candle as well as incense to waft smoke in front of a statue of Buddha, put on some inspirational chant music, then sat in front of my computer at an antique Chinese writing desk. I was ready to write.

As I began, I recalled a statement my mother used to say to me. It went something like this: "Work hard and you will reap." Her words served as the foundation of my speech.

I realized the meaning of this statement had always remained something of a mystery to me. What had she meant? Was it a metaphor for a deeper truth? Many words flashed in my mind as I contemplated the speech, including "expectations," "showing-up," "essence," "effort," "reward," "results," "renaissance," and "reinvention."

As I developed the initial structure of my speech, I realized that I have changed my life every decade, essentially reinventing myself in exciting and often unexpected ways every ten years. The speech then became a "fly-over" of sorts of each decade of my life.

From this metaphoric bird's-eye view, I opened with the following: "With all my love and in profound respect to you, my audience, I welcome you to the abridged version of my life. Work hard and you will reap."

I envisioned standing before my audience, raising my left arm, and saying, "To my left is my past, where I stand is my present, and to my right, the future.

"My life has been characterized by elite performance and a constant striving for personal excellence. I have been a figure skater, a dancer, choreographer, director, short-film director, and now, I am a professional coach, trainer, and a respected motivational speaker. I have lived in thirteen cities, on three continents, and lived in well over thirty-four homes and apartments. At times, I feel like I've compacted several lifetimes into one."

I continued to write and get into the body of the speech. The first decade of my life I entitled "Growing Up." My life began in a logging camp called "Caycuse Camp" near Lake Cowichan, on Vancouver Island, Canada. I spent many glorious months at Caycuse during the first five years of my life, and also many glorious summers thereafter, when we moved south to the city of Victoria. I fondly remember these years of bliss and playfulness as a youngster in nature. I would swim with friends, water-ski, discover tadpoles and watch them grow into frogs, log roll, and run on the "lily pads" (horizontal cuts of trees that are floated in log booms on the water), as well as many other activities that formed my early years.

In Victoria, I went to school and began to figure skate. The second decade of my life, I called "Champion." This decade referred to the life I led studying, becoming an honour roll student, and training many long hours to become a Junior National Ice Dance Champion in Canada. I dedicated the majority of my time during this period solely to sport and studying. Whenever I didn't win in skating or get an award at school, my mother would say, "Work hard and you will reap." With these words, I continued on.

However, many times I felt there were injustices in my life. For example, I was the most gifted skater in my club but didn't receive awards for my efforts. Another time, I was given an award at school, only for it to be later taken away from me for some unknown reason. I couldn't understand this, but my mother kept repeating the same statement. Of course, at that time I had yet to learn its deeper truth. At the end of my second decade, I stopped competitive skating. I was bitter when I left the competitive scene and began to disbelieve in my mother's statement. I had expectations in skating, but unfortunately they didn't come to complete fruition due to the scene's politics and our lack of money to continue.

My third decade became known as "Knowledge, Training, Performing." I realized somewhere in those early years of my twenties that I was moving into a period of self-discovery. I didn't want to be confined to the rigours of my narrow world of skating. I wanted to set my wings free and fly away. I did, and flew to Australia to teach figure skating. I couldn't have been much farther away from the skating scene of Canada.

In this third decade, I travelled around the world; received a biology degree at university, prepared for medical school, but decided not to apply; bought a house; and lived in Paris, New York City, and Ottawa. It was fantastic decade of learning.

As I burst into my fourth decade, integrating my dance, skating, performance, and science backgrounds, my mother's words returned to my mind from time to time. I called my fourth decade "Flavour of the Month." In this period, I was on a meteoric rise in the international figure skating world as a well-known and gifted choreographer. I worked with many national, world, and Olympic champions and other competitors from various countries on choreography for different purposes. I attended world championships with my students; taught ice theatre and dance classes; lived in Ottawa, Toronto, Calgary, and Edmonton; travelled extensively; and was sought out by numerous artistic and sports organizations to choreograph and teach workshops on creativity.

My crowning achievement in this period was to choreograph and direct the closing ceremonies for the 1988 Calgary Winter Olympic

Games. It was a very fruitful decade in which I received many accolades, extensive coverage in the national and international press, and numerous and noteworthy successes. However, again I ended the decade with more changes in my life.

My mother's words kept ringing inside me, especially when the going got rough, and it did at times, as nothing is ever that smooth. At this point, I began to really question the meaning of my mother's words. I thought she must have been misinformed. Working hard doesn't necessarily mean you will reap the rewards. But what was the truth behind all of this?

Regardless of my disenchantment with my mother's words, I entered my fifth decade full of vigour. I entitled it "Realization." I continued to work hard, achieve, and do my best at whatever I did. However, something told me to take a step outside for a moment and look at the world of skating and my life. I asked myself, "Do you want to still be standing on cold ice rinks when you are fifty, sixty, or even older?" And a voice emphatically replied, "No." With that, I realized I wanted more from my life. I decided to give myself ten more years, until I was fifty, to reinvent myself once again. I set out to explore my passions again. I knew I loved photography as a teenager and had an eye for shapes and forms. It led me to thinking about movement, elite performance, and photography. Film came to mind. While I continued to work in skating, creating some wonderful projects, such as international touring shows, I embarked on carving out a career in dance filmmaking. This led to the creation of a number of award-winning dance films under my direction, which was very exciting indeed.

In my forties, I also realized I was becoming more philosophical about life in general, and this was extremely appealing to me. I thought there must be some greater aspect to life that I was not realizing. During this period, I proceeded through great deal of turmoil, internally and externally. I went from creative devastation to loss of my self-confidence, and hit the lowest parts of my life, but I bounced back and hit some of the highest points in my life as well. The greatest positive note of this period was my awakening to my inner self and the learning that goes with this part of the journey.

Somehow, I sensed skating was leaving me, and before I knew it, it came to an abrupt halt when I was forty-eight. I couldn't believe it, but then that is what I had asked for in my early forties and now it was here. I just didn't feel it would end without a ceremonious goodbye or something like that. It just ended. Through this and other events in my life, I have come to realize that I have to be careful what I ask the universe for, because it may very likely happen and perhaps not in the way I had planned.

My sixth decade of my life flew in, "Re-Invention." This period started with me living in Brussels where I had moved in order to re-invent myself. It proved itself to be a tough journey. Luckily, with the support and grace of my good friends Bojan and Robin, I was eventually able to move out of that tough situation. My mother's words flew back into my being during this difficult period, when lack of money was the norm in that early decade. Again, for the life of me, I couldn't see any positive intention in "work hard and you will reap."

Then I met a wonderful personal coach while designing a friend's wedding in Spain. She became my coach and got me through this period of transition with grace. The result of our sessions is the man I am today. I am now an inspirational coach, facilitator, and speaker, specializing in the areas of energy management, values, and well-being. Coaching is where I have found I can give, receive, and be in my life for the next decade, at least, before I begin to possibly reinvent another life situation.

As I continued to write my Toastmaster's speech on that chilly, early winter morning, an epiphany appeared before me: "To my left is my past, where I stand before you is my present, and to my right, my future." As

I said this, it hit me, eureka! My mother's words were about truth—the pearl, truth. For years, I had been clearly seeing and experiencing only a literal meaning and manifestation of her saying. What I was missing was the deeper heart message, the internal meaning, the metaphor in life. When she would say these words to me, she was probably not thinking of this at the time, but deep inside of her I sensed another voice was speaking.

I have come to realize that with all the knowledge and learning we undertake, awareness, deep awareness, can only happen when the time is right. It happens when the energetic factors of the internal and external collide and an epiphany or *Aha* moment appears. The lessons may come one at a time or many at a time, but it's how you align, integrate, and put them into action that will lead to transformation.

As I wrote my speech, I came to realize that for decades I had been expecting things to happen from one point of view. It was my point of view of what I should "reap." For me, reaping was an external gratification only made possible by material objects, accolades, press reviews, and money. When I reflected on this, there were many times when I was not listening to the voice inside of me, to my heart and intuition. My perception was that morally, if I do work hard I should be materially rewarded for it. This is true sometimes, but it is not the only reward.

I had somehow discounted that I was indeed rewarded for everything I had done and was rewarded in many ways. I was living on the surface of my skin. I was seeing and experiencing life only from my ego. For the most part, I simply didn't have a deeply balanced or healthy knowledge and attitude about myself.

I had been lost in the cacophony of the physical and mental aspects of my existence, which often were like disconnected pieces of a puzzle. What I was missing were the connections. I was not fully recognizing or listening to my real Self. I had drowned out my spiritual voice even when it was screaming for me. Yes, there were definitely *Aha* moments of awareness. They would often appear very far apart at first, and now, I find they are occurring on an ongoing basis.

Something else happened that early morning which began to connect the dots in my life. That is when "truth" arose, alive and well. I finally was able to give myself permission to accept my life honestly, in its total fullness. I realized that to "work" is to take action and to "reap" the rewards is truth. I was now reaping something more profound than I had ever expected.

Finally, I had begun to reap the benefits of all the tangible and intangible events in my life, as well as the journey to my soul. I was able to further recognise that all the action I had taken in life was leading me to pure learning and knowledge, the truth about life. My epiphany was so simple. It had been staring me in the face all along, for so many decades; I was just preoccupied by looking in a different direction. Finally, I, the student, was ready to listen from the heart.

When I finished writing my speech, the sun was about to rise. The sun rose within me as well. My mother gave me a pearl that was wise and profound. It may have taken many decades to realize it, but so be it. The most important point in life is to become aware, realize, and actively choose to live the truth.

So, when I remembered my mother's words, "Work hard and you will reap," I again lifted my left arm, and gleefully gazed on my past five decades. I saw the truth and felt a sense of harmony and contentment in the present. I blissfully looked to right, my future, with a new state of awareness of my entire being. I put my pen down and with a smile on my face and the sun of truth in my heart, I decided to go back to bed for a little nap.

DISCOVERY

Have you found the truth in your life? ~ What is truth to you? ~ How do you manifest truth? ~ What can understanding and living your truth do for you? ~ Give yourself permission to be alive and seek to understand your innermost truth. "Work hard and you will reap." Believe in your truth and put it into action, now!

Epilogue

To my mother and the mother within us all.

I thank my mother for her biggest pearl of all, truth.
Whether it was her intention or not,
I accept this as her greatest gift and
lesson for me in her life.
It has taken me five decades to realize this and
many of us will come to it
at our own pace and time in life.
Others may not,
but here is your chance, now.
Through sharing this with you
my wish
is that it won't take as long for you as it did me.
But again, life plays tricks on us and
when the student is ready
the teacher will appear.
Stand on guard,
be alert, and
keep that door open,
your senses piqued, and
be ready to move when awareness strikes,
as it may be a fleeting moment.
Grasp it,
run with it,
dance with joy, and
forever be grateful that
this is the bigger picture of life.
The reason you are here,
is to seek the truth,
through your own stories.

With all my love and respect, I welcome you to your Mother's Pearls.